CONTEMPORARIES
and
SNOBS

MODERN AND CONTEMPORARY POETICS

Series Editors
Charles Bernstein
Hank Lazer

Series Advisory Board
Maria Damon
Rachel Blau DuPlessis
Alan Golding
Susan Howe
Nathaniel Mackey
Jerome McGann
Harryette Mullen
Aldon Nielsen
Marjorie Perloff
Joan Retallack
Ron Silliman
Jerry Ward

CONTEMPORARIES
and
SNOBS

Laura Riding

Edited by Laura Heffernan and Jane Malcolm

The University of Alabama Press
Tuscaloosa

Introduction, supplemental notes, bibliography, and index copyright © 2014
The University of Alabama Press
Tuscaloosa, Alabama 35487-0380
All rights reserved
Manufactured in the United States of America

Contemporaries and Snobs © Cornell University Library
First published 1928. Restored © owned by Division of Rare and Manuscript Collections, Cornell University Library.

Typeface: Minion and Futura

Cover image: Courtesy of Laura Heffernan and Jane Malcolm.
Cover design: Mary Elizabeth Watson

∞

The paper on which this book is printed meets the minimum requirements of American National Standard for Information Sciences—Permanence of Paper for Printed Library Materials, ANSI Z39.48-1984.

Library of Congress Cataloging-in-Publication Data

Riding, Laura, 1901–1991.
Contemporaries and snobs / Laura Riding ; edited by Laura Heffernan and Jane Malcolm.
pages cm. — (Modern and contemporary poetics)
Originally published: Garden City, N.Y.: Doubleday Doran, 1928.
Includes bibliographical references and index.
ISBN 978-0-8173-5767-2 (quality paper : alk. paper) — ISBN 978-0-8173-8737-2 (e book) 1. Poetry. I. Heffernan, Laura, editor. II. Malcolm, Jane editor. III. Title.
PN1136.J27 2014
808.1—dc23

2013030768

Contents

Acknowledgments vii

We Must Be Barbaric: An Introduction to *Contemporaries and Snobs* ix

1. Poetry and the Literary Universe 1

I. Shame of the Person 1

II. Poetry, Out of Employment, Writes on Unemployment 5

III. Escapes from the Zeitgeist 10

IV. Poetic Reality and Critical Unreality 21

V. Poetry and Progress 31

VI. The Higher Snobbism 39

2. T. E. Hulme, the New Barbarism, and Gertrude Stein 51

3. The Facts in the Case of Monsieur Poe 86

Editors' Notes 113

Chronological Bibliography 123

Index 127

Acknowledgments

We would like to thank the Division of Rare and Manuscript Collections, Carl A. Kroch Library, Cornell University for their assistance. Elizabeth Friedmann's knowledge of Laura Riding's life and letters is vast, and she provided us with crucial insight at key stages of our research. Charles Bernstein and Josephine Park were our earliest readers and supporters. Our thanks also to Jeremy Braddock, Lisa Samuels, and Rachel Buurma for their help along the way.

We Must Be Barbaric

An Introduction to *Contemporaries and Snobs*

Laura Heffernan and Jane Malcolm

> I was, as a poet, an inveterate propounder of a necessity of non-distinction between person and poet.
>
> —Laura (Riding) Jackson, "An Autobiographical Summary"

Laura Riding's *Contemporaries and Snobs*, first published in 1928, drew a line down the center of the literary scene in the late 1920s. With characteristic incisiveness, Riding divided friends from foes: she counted as enemies those "snobs," or critics, who sought to systematize and professionalize modern poetry. As allies, Riding counted all "contemporaries" who continued to honor poetry as an individual and eccentric practice. Yet Riding's bold and uncongenial treatise was not merely a call to arms in and of the modernist moment. For readers today, it offers a compelling account—by turns personal, by turns historical—of how the institutionalization of modernism denuded experimental poetry. Most importantly, *Contemporaries* offers a counter history of the idiosyncratic, of what the institution of modernism left (and leaves) behind. With Gertrude Stein as its figurehead, the book champions the non-canonical, the "barbaric," and the under-theorized. Riding's nuanced defense of a poetics of the person in *Contemporaries* represents a forgotten but essential first attempt to identify and foster what is now a well-defined poetic lineage that leads from Stein to the experimental avant-garde.

Riding began writing *Contemporaries* in 1926, but the book did not appear until early 1928. The latter half of the 1920s was a prolific period for Riding. Her *A Survey of Modernist Poetry*, written with Robert Graves, appeared in late 1927, followed by *Contemporaries* in February of 1928, *Anarchism Is Not Enough* (the creative sequel to *Contemporaries*) in May, and *A Pamphlet Against Anthologies* (also written with Graves) in July. *Contemporaries* is the most ignored of this varied bunch, perhaps because it responds so directly to the criticism and poetry of its moment. Riding takes her readers on a remarkably thorough tour through the "self-critical, severe, sophisticated" literary scene of the 1920s (53). Among other influential treatises, she considers T. S. Eliot's *The Sacred Wood* and his editorial essays in *The Criterion*, Allen Tate's "Poetry and the Absolute," John Crowe Ransom's essays on the modernist poet, Edgell Rickword's essays in *The Calendar of Modern Letters*, and Herbert Read's posthumous publication of T. E. Hulme's essays.

All of this criticism, Riding notes, gave modern poets a sheen of seriousness and professionalism, but was it good for poetry? Her decisive answer is "no." Poets, taking their marching orders from criticism, had begun to churn out deadened, impersonal poetry that gave voice to an imagined "zeitgeist" rather than individual experience. *Contemporaries* was Riding's attempt to stem this tide—to resist the consolidation of poetic experimentalism into monolithic modernism. Not only a critical diatribe, *Contemporaries* was also a self-help manual for those poets who wished to write "outside the shelter of contemporary criticism" (4). To sustain these "incorruptible individuals," Riding builds a purely provisional canon of poets as persons, writers who use language to sense the unknown (4). Her perceptive reading of Stein forms the cornerstone of this revaluation of the personal in poetry, and she uses the example of Stein's "barbaric" writing to question the very process of self-representation that language—Stein's "arrangement in a system to pointing"—makes possible (*Tender Buttons* 245). At a moment when poet-critics were offering poets a loaded choice between naive expressionism and sophisticated impersonality, Riding denounced both as escapist. As modernism turned self-referentially inward, *Contemporaries* forged a pathway outward toward newly referential uses of language, toward an unknown and unsanctioned poetry of the person.

From *A Survey of Modernist Poetry* to *Contemporaries and Snobs*

Riding was better situated than most to reflect on modernism's condensation. By 1928, she had come into contact with an astonishing number of modernist groups in Nashville, New York, London, and Paris. As an early member of John Crowe Ransom's Fugitive Group in Nashville, she befriended Allen Tate and Robert Penn Warren. Her poetry first appeared in the pages of *The Fugitive* in 1923 and later in Harriet Monroe's Chicago-based *Poetry: A Magazine of Verse*. In 1925, Riding moved from Louisville to Greenwich Village where she befriended Hart Crane and met Eugene O'Neill, Edmund Wilson, and Kenneth Burke. While in New York, Riding corresponded with Robert Graves who had written in admiration of her poem "The Quids." She soon moved to England to live with Graves and his wife, Nancy Nicholson. Riding and Graves's collaboration (and eventual romantic relationship) continued throughout the 1920s, when they moved between Egypt, Islip, Vienna,

Hammersmith, Germany, Paris, and Mallorca. During this time, Riding published creative work with Leonard and Virginia Woolf's Hogarth Press, was introduced to Gertrude Stein, exchanged work with Wyndham Lewis, and contributed essays to Eugene Jolas's Joyce-centric little magazine *transition*. Of the three essays collected in *Contemporaries*, two had debuted in other venues. The second chapter and core of the book, "T. E. Hulme, the New Barbarism, and Gertrude Stein," was published in *transition* in 1927 as "The New Barbarism and Gertrude Stein," and again, in altered form, as the "Conclusion" to *A Survey of Modernist Poetry*, while a version of the volume's third chapter, "The Facts in the Case of Monsieur Poe," appeared in *transition* as "Jamais Plus" and was given as a talk to the undergraduate Oxford English Club in March of 1927 (Friedmann 102).

Riding herself was one of the first critics to coin the term "modernist" to describe a group of contemporary poets, and she and Graves are cited accordingly in the Oxford English Dictionary's entry. Their *A Survey of Modernist Poetry* (1927) was the first formal study to consider the work of E. E. Cummings, Hart Crane, Conrad Aiken, Marianne Moore, Ezra Pound, Vachel Lindsay, T. S. Eliot, John Crowe Ransom, Edith Sitwell, and Allen Tate as a single movement. In that volume, Riding and Graves set out to consider whether the "plain reader" was justified in his complaint that the modernist "poet means to keep the public out" (*Survey* 10). Selecting a few representative examples of modern poetry, Riding and Graves carefully considered the significance of the poems' format, or the ways in which their radical formal departures, viewed together, came to signify a new modernist poetry. Through such close interpretations Riding and Graves modeled how the plain reader might "make certain important alterations in his critical attitude" in order to appreciate Cummings as much as Shakespeare, John Crowe Ransom as much as Wordsworth (10).

Though *Survey of Modernist Poetry* defends modernist poets from charges of willful obscurity, Riding and Graves resisted the urge to put forward an overarching definition or theory of modernism. Indeed, we can already see in that volume the beginnings of Riding's fears that poetic theories were overtaking poetry. In frequent asides, the *Survey* warns poets about the danger of "granting too much respect to theories" or committing oneself to the "official programmes of such dead movements as Imagism" and expresses disdain for those "who need the support of a system" or adopt one as a way of "attempting to justify [poetry] to civilization" (*Survey* 126). In the "Conclusion" to *Survey*, a version of Chapter 2 of *Contemporaries*, Riding and Graves jettison the "contemporary sympathy" they have shown for modernist poetry in order to consider it as a movement that "may have already passed":

> We have been writing as it were from the middle of the modernist movement in order to justify it if possible against criticism which was not proper to it. . . . It is now possible to reach a position where the modernist movement itself can be looked at with historical (as opposed to contemporary) sympathy as a stage in poetry that is to pass in turn, or may have already passed, leaving behind only such work as did not belong too much to history. (258)

Here, at the end of *Survey*, we see Riding and Graves "leaving" modernism "behind": no longer defending it from the inside, they now scrutinize it from the outside.

Contemporaries extends this newly skeptical perspective on a "modernist movement" that, having just come into clear view, now seems about to "pass in turn." Indeed, the modernism of *Contemporaries* is markedly different from that of *Survey*. Where *Survey* presented close readings of individual poems, *Contemporaries* takes a distant, multicentury view of modernism's development. Where *Survey* presented modernism as "unpopular" with contemporary critics and readers, *Contemporaries* finds evidence everywhere of modernism's newfound prestige, even—perhaps especially—among the mainstream press and the middle classes. From the suburban Bournemouth Poetry Society's advertisement for a "paper by Mrs. Leslie Goodwin on 'Further Aspects of Modern Poetry,'" to the fact that the *London Mercury* dares not question [T. S. Eliot's] *The New Criterion*, (28) to the way Eliot's poems become instant classics upon their publication, all signs point to the sanctification of modernism—a status that seems, in *Contemporaries*, as ill-deserved as its negative reputation seemed in *Survey* (29, 28).

One way to understand the drastic shift in perspective between the two volumes is to consider that modernism's new recognition and popularity did not extend to Riding herself. Having once felt herself working in concert with many modernist groups and owing allegiance to none, Riding suddenly found herself an onlooker to the mainstream of modernism—a mainstream dominated by male critics. Indeed, Riding begins a 1927 letter to Wyndham Lewis by explaining: "I belong (most decidedly) to no group." Reviewers (most famously, William Empson) repeatedly failed to credit Riding as co-author of *Survey*, despite Graves's insistence that their collaboration had been "word by word" (Friedmann 100). Riding's correspondence from this era, preserved in the Laura (Riding) Jackson archive at Cornell University, documents her dogged attempts to make publishers and authors responsible for their errors of attribution.

Riding's archive tells a similarly bleak tale about the publication and reception of *Contemporaries*. Though the book was a solo effort (written over several years and for various venues), Graves traded on his own success to secure its publication: when Jonathan Cape sought to publish Graves's popular biography of T. E. Lawrence, *Lawrence and the Arabs* (1927), Graves made it a condition of his contract that they also publish *Contemporaries* (Friedmann 107). In 1933, Riding's publisher wrote to request her permission to remainder the unsold copies from the modest print run of *Contemporaries*. Indeed, the volume was so under-read that no one would bat an eyelash two years later when Geoffrey West matter-of-factly adopted Riding's own opposition between the "philosophical" criticism of T. E. Hulme and T. S. Eliot on the one hand and Stein's writing on the other, in order to dismiss Riding herself. In *Deucalion: Or the Future of Literary Criticism*, written for Kegan Paul's To-Day and To-Morrow series, West announced that "philosophical critics" like T. E. Hulme and T. S. Eliot were "of greatest importance" to the future of literary criticism, "while reference may . . . be omitted to such isolated, unrelated phenomena as the smoky brilliances of Miss Rebecca West and the ultra-feminine Steinish incoherencies of Miss Laura Riding" (48–49).

Despite the chauvinism that Riding faced, *Contemporaries* hardly reads like a personal complaint, nor does the gossipy feel of the title extend to the essays. Graves wrote to T. S. Eliot in 1926 that "her critical detachment is certainly greater than mine" (qtd. Friedmann 78). Instead, *Contemporaries* offers perhaps the most distanced, historical analysis possible of how and why Riding's fellow modernists traded their individuality for the security of a professional institution. And though Riding advocates, in *Contemporaries*, for a poetics of the "person," the volume's voice is hardly personable. Riding insists that readers understand her embrace of Stein and a poetics of the person not as feminist revaluations but as matter-of-fact corrections to modernists' symptomatic, even effeminate, attempts to escape from personality. Indeed, it is Riding's own detachment, imperiousness, and misogynist mudslinging that makes *Contemporaries* such a fascinating document—a critical book that denounces criticism's growing influence. (The self-contradictions of Riding's position would only increase. After denouncing critical organs like *The Criterion* in *Contemporaries*, Riding would in 1935 found *Epilogue*, a little magazine which, as Joyce Wexler has documented, Riding edited with an iron fist in an attempt to institutionalize her very particular point of view.) These paradoxical positions, perhaps even more than Riding's specific argument, reveal a moment in which the range of avant-garde possibilities seemed suddenly whittled down into equally distasteful options: to become an "affiliated member" (53) of modernism, which held a monopoly on intellectual seriousness, or to find oneself shelved with the book-club "poetry enthusiasts" (29).

The Argument of Contemporaries and Snobs

The opening sections of *Contemporaries* offer a broad historical account of how the rise of scientific empiricism has gradually marginalized poetry. Crucially for Riding, science and poetry are equal forms of knowledge but with different orientations to the world. Science uses what Riding terms "concrete intelligence," which "regards everything as potentially comprehensible and measurable" (5). In contrast, "poetic intelligence" evinces "an accurate sensation of the unknown, an inspired comprehension of the unknowable" (5). Centuries ago, Riding argues, the two coexisted without rancor—each occupying its own "corner of human knowledge" (33). But over the course of the nineteenth century, which "showed a more material increase than perhaps any other preceding century in this mass-consciousness of human knowledge," scientific empiricism began to take precedence and to popularize the false idea that all life might be measured and known (7). Riding describes, for instance, how concrete intelligence gives birth to "natural man," a scientific specimen "who did not act originally; he did not act at all. It was his function to be observed" (2). This passive, statistical version of man takes the place of the "erratic person," upon whose activity and unknowability poetry had thrived.

Turning to the twentieth century, Riding describes how poetry has gradually become ashamed of itself. In the face of natural man, it develops a distaste for idiosyncrasy and a "shame of the person" (11); in the face of concrete intelligence, it ceases to regard its "illuminating ignorance" as a species of knowledge at all (1, 5). Riding's metaphors suggest that poets, within a rationalized modernity, have come to seem like unprofitable workers: society gives poetry its "dismissal papers" (28) and "Poetry, Out of Employment, Writes on Unemployment" (5). Like underemployed workers, poets begin to reflect upon their social position, develop a collective consciousness, and unionize in order to put themselves back to work. Riding describes how individual poets have, increasingly in the twentieth-century, gathered together under the auspices of the "public institution" of literary criticism. Rather than looking to their own erratic personhood for poetic inspiration, they look now to the collective, critical mandates of their time. Yet in the inhospitable atmosphere of rationalized modernity, these critical mandates have themselves become increasingly directive and systematized. Riding likens poetry to any organization—"the army, or the navy, for example"—that introduces "greater internal discipline" when its "prestige . . . is curtailed" (53).

In the remainder of Chapter 1 and in Chapter 2, Riding looks to the modernist literature and criticism around her to offer an astonishing array of examples of literary culture's increased discipline. She describes a new injunction to "write about nothing" or about the death of poetry itself (as in Edwin Muir's *Chorus of the Newly Dead* or Eliot's *The Hollow Men*) (8). She detects a new scholastic tendency to look back on the literature of the past as a continuous "tradition." (She points here, among other things, to James Joyce's "Oxen of the Sun" episode of *Ulysses* in which Joyce provides a catalogue of past literary styles.) Reviewing the table of contents for one issue of Eliot's *The New Criterion*, Riding finds a new love of "pedigree, learning and literary internationalism" (25). She describes a new "emphasis on the medium as material," as in Ezra Pound's book on the sculptor *Gaudier-Brzeska* (72). She notes a new imperative for poets to express the "Zietgeist" to the point of "self-extinction," as in Eliot's "posthumous" poetry or Edith Sitwell's "strict technical organization of her non-humanistic universe" (9). Above all, she finds a new philosophical inquiry into the function of poetry itself—Allen Tate's philosophizing about "Poetry and the Absolute," Pound's "mathematical and geometric" metaphors, Eliot's insistence that "in our time the most vigorous critical minds are philosophical minds," and everyone's elevation of T. E. Hulme's "barbaric" criticism into a dogmatic philosophy of art (75, 25, 63). Riding regards all of the above as signs of the increasing and pernicious influence of literary criticism, which seeks to present poets as serious specialists and thus to win back a modicum of status from an uninterested society: "The reason why contemporary critics are so interested in inquiring into the nature of the function of literature is not, as Mr. Eliot suggests, because they do not wish 'to take for granted a whole universe', but because a whole universe has given literature its dismissal papers" (28).

For Riding, then, the danger of this "forced" systematism is that it has begun to change how poets write. A "group poetic mind," the book argues, lurks "at the elbow of the individual poet," preventing him from writing authentically because he is burdened by a self-referential network of modernist institutions that dictate the terms of poetic composition (54). A "professional conscience dawns on the poet," creation and criticism become folded into a single act (as Eliot had predicted), and the poet begins to edit himself in the process of writing (53). The results, in Riding's view, are disastrous: homogeneous, vacant poetry that is "really more interested in maintaining a defensive attitude toward the literary past than in sponsoring a 'new' poetry" (4). Riding mentions a few poets—Arthur Rimbaud, Robert Graves, and Hart Crane, for example—who have succeeded in avoiding these mandates, but the vast majority have succumbed to the imperative to write impersonally.

Impersonality/Personality

Riding's preoccupation with the dangers of impersonality critically shapes the argument in *Contemporaries*. The rise of an impersonal aesthetic and the waning of emotion in modernist poetry are, for Riding, symptomatic of an ironic romanticism, a need to "suppress the obvious because the obvious is often romantically (personally), therefore sentimentally beautiful" (70). Unlike many of her contemporaries, she did not believe that the surrender of meaning or the disappearance of the personal signaled bold shifts in literary practice. On the contrary, Riding argues throughout *Contemporaries* that poets who disavow their own "vulgar humanity" (75) are in fact ashamed of it and of the emotions that shape their "organic existence" as poets:

> It is romantic to say, while denouncing as romantic the meanings which the creative mind gives to its fictions, that these can only be valid if they confess their meaninglessness. Is not a belief in the lack of meaning in organic existence merely a new meaning that art is to adopt for the sake of the prestige given it by the metaphysics from which it is drawn? (68)

Poets who "confess their meaninglessness," to a certain extent do so in order to avoid the shame and human difficulty of modernity, which for Riding are precisely the realms poetry should confront.

Riding's seemingly anachronistic reclamation of the person, of the poet as person, evinces her supreme ambivalence about modernism, and her reasons for promoting a poetics of personality are as fascinating as they are complex. Poets, Riding insists, might shed the "classical desideratum" of mentors likes Eliot and Pound by embracing emotion, personality, and embodied language as a condition of their art, so that poetry might tell the truth (70). Yet this definition of poetry seems contrary to the very underpinnings of modernism—the unstable "I," the erased ego, the elevation of language over subject. Riding, whose own *Survey* coined the term "modernist" to describe a generation of poets invested in suppressing the "I," declares that poetry should be personal, that we cannot "substitute poetics for persons" (47). This statement is perhaps the best condensation of Riding's argument in *Contemporaries*, the closest the book comes to providing a rallying cry for her fellow poets. As a thesis it is controversial, to say the least, and in this respect, *Contemporaries* seeks to refute Eliot's key assertion, in "Tradition and the Individual Talent" (1919), that "poetry is not a turning loose of emotion, but is an escape from emotion; it is not the expression of personality, but an escape from personality" (*Sacred Wood* 58). If Eliot welcomes impersonality as a creative reprieve, Riding laments it and the "general degradation of the person" as the compromised methodology of institutional modernism that "set about . . . exterminating the person" as a matter of aesthetics (68). Riding sees in this methodology a deeply rooted fear of innovation and understands the reluctance to produce truly new poetry as the inevitable result of a group mentality.

Throughout *Contemporaries*, Riding portrays poetic impersonality as the warped outcome of an intensely felt shame of the person. Thus, for instance, she depicts Eliot's desire to "escape from emotion" and "escape from personality" as childish, effeminate, and fearful. Calling *The Waste Land* the "great twentieth-century nursery rhyme" (45), she argues that, by avoiding emotion, or as in Eliot's theory of the "objective correlative," displacing the weight of emotions onto objects rather than subjects, the poet compels his readers to engage in psychologically driven close readings, mining the poem for evidence of authorial trauma (45). Hard modernism, she explains, should confront humanity (a dangerously amorphous entity) in all of its emotional complexity. The poet as person should not seek to sever personality from poetics. Accordingly, Riding refers to Eliot, Joyce, and Co. collectively as "ladies" precisely because they "avoid the temptations to sentimentality inherent in the poetic faculty" and thus reject the humanity inherent in their medium, language (48). Riding's ironic use of gender demonstrates the depth of her scorn for the calculated modernist (im)persona, even as it suggests that we should understand her reclamation of the poet as person not as the romantic agenda of an iconoclast woman modernist, but as the cornerstone of a grittier, more authentic, and truly hard (both difficult and obdurate) poetics in and of the modernist moment. Why insist upon and theorize the "'difficulty' of modernist poetry," Riding asks, when "well-written poetry is always difficult" (54)?

Riding's ideal poet, then, displays true originality by refusing to reflect a shared modernist dogma, by casting aside a poetics of impersonality, and by acknowledging language itself as a unique medium (and burden), one "to accept . . . from humanity at large" (57). Indeed, Riding's poetics of the person emerges in precisely this matter-of-fact way, as a kind of recognition and reminder that the poet and poetic language remain always embedded in unsystematized life. As Lisa Samuels explains, Riding "is always personal and always looking for unfoldings of what the self cannot quite conceive" (*Anarchism is Not Enough* xi). For Riding, the "person" behind a poem cannot ever be "exterminated." Poets are persons always, not persons when life is messy and poets when they are at work on clean and sharp angles. Nor does Riding's emphasis on the person arise from a lyric expressivism in which poetry emanates from the poetic mind. Rather, good poets, for Riding, stand in a respectful and somewhat diminutive relation to their relatively independent poems: "The poem itself is supreme, above persons; judging rather than judged; keeping criticism at a respectful distance; it is even able to make a reader of its author" (23). In *A Survey of Modernist Poetry*, Riding and Graves likened the relation between a poet and his poem to the relationship between a "wise, experimenting parent" and child. Just as a parent would not wish to keep a child in "its place" by "suppressing its personality or laughing down its strange questions, so that it turns into a rather dull and ineffective edition of the parent," poets are likewise "freeing the poem" and "encouraging it to do things, even queer things, by itself" (124–125). Riding continues this logic in *Contemporaries*, arguing that the role of poetry is to create "an ever immediate reality confirmed afresh and independently in each new work," a reality "confirmed personally rather than professionally" (56). Only by fostering this relation of connection and freedom can poets write poems that are not mere copies of what already exists, but that bring, out of language, something new into being.

Gertrude Stein and the "New Barbarism"

Contemporaries finds its ambassador of the everyday, its poet as person, in Gertrude Stein. Riding first became familiar with Stein's work in 1926 when the Hogarth Press published her own collection of poems, *The Close Chaplet*, as well as Stein's "Composition as Explanation," a text whose influence in *Contemporaries* cannot be underestimated. Riding began writing about Stein in *Survey*, and the two became friends and frequent correspondents after "The New Barbarism and Gertrude Stein" appeared in the June 1927 issue of *transition*. (Stein was understandably pleased to have been so thoroughly championed by Riding.) That essay prompted Stein to send Riding and Graves a manuscript version of *An Acquaintance With Description*, which their Seizin Press published in 1929. The intensity of their relationship during these years, particularly as reflected in Riding's letters, translates into an equally intense critical devotion in Chapter 2 of *Contemporaries*, in which Riding explains and lauds Stein's "barbarism."

As a continuation of her essay in *transition*, the Stein chapter clearly responds to Eliot's ominous denunciation of Stein in "Charleston, Hey! Hey!," a review written for *Nation & Athenaeum* in January 1927: "[Stein's] work is not improving, it is not amusing, it is not interesting, it is not good for one's mind. But its rhythms have a peculiar hypnotic power not met with before. It has a kinship with the saxophone. If this is the future, then the future is, as it very likely is, of the barbarians. But this is the future in which we ought not to be interested" (595). Riding seizes upon the word "barbarians," upending Eliot's dismissive analogy, and proceeds to sketch out a positive poetics of barbarism in *Contemporaries* (66). Riding argues that by "taking everything around her very literally and many things for granted which others have not been naive enough to take so," Stein has fundamentally altered poetic modernism (78). She insists that "no one but Miss Stein has been willing to be as ordinary, as simple, as primitive, as stupid, as barbaric as successful barbarism demands," and that Stein, by doing "what everyone else has been ashamed to do," is the only modernist whose compositions are firmly rooted in the everyday (78). Because Stein writes so far outside the generic parameters of her contemporaries, Riding argues, she has managed to achieve authenticity, while at the same time subverting modernism's prestige-obsessed institutions: "She has courage, clarity, sincerity, simplicity. She has created a human mean in language, a mathematical equation of ordinariness, which leaves one with a tender respect for that changing and unchanging slowness that is humanity and Gertrude Stein" (84). If Stein is a "barbaric" writer, or if, as Eliot warns, she is "going to make trouble for us," for Riding this trouble will be the salvation of the avant-garde.

At least one reviewer of *Contemporaries* recognized that Riding was attempting, through a revaluation of Stein, to radically redefine poetic practice for the modernist moment. A 1928 *Times Literary Supplement* review finds merit in Riding's preoccupation with the person and in her insistence that "poetry should be a humanity" (254). As a treatise "riding on the backs" (pun certainly intended) of contemporary poets, the reviewer argues, *Contemporaries* articulates a much needed theory of poetic practice wedded to personal language and the commonplace, to the "apples and napkins of poetry, associations of which no poet should be queasy" (254). Riding does indeed extol the "apples and napkins of poetry," both in her insistence that poetry cannot be divorced from everyday language, and in her theorization of Stein's radical poetics. Professional modernists, Riding argues, try to make language an external medium—like paint to the painter or stone to the sculptor. In so doing, modernists transform poetry into a specialist discipline—a rigidly defined cultural production, one "Art" among others. As Jerome McGann puts it, Riding replaced modernism's vision of poetry as "an art of making" (which she saw as an evasion of "what is most human about the way we use language") with a vision of poetry as an art "of telling" (McGann 313). Returning, as Stein does in *Tender Buttons*, to the apples and napkins—the everyday and everywhere of language—Riding reinvents the poet as person and sets the terms for a poetic practice that grapples with the uncertainties of language and personhood.

Above all, Riding and Stein both value particularity, and Riding uses the Stein chapter in *Contemporaries* to argue for the everyday singularity of poetic language in the hands of the poet as person. Stein's influence is most evident in the pages devoted to the "time-sense," as Riding's own exposition and locution begin to echo the recursive diction in "Composition as Explanation." Much like Stein's often quoted adage, "everything is the same except composition and time, composition and the time of the composition and the time in the composition" (500), Riding's definition of the "time-sense" is derived from her own understanding of Steinian language: "The composition is clear because the language means nothing but what it means in her using of it" (82). Stein's version of modernist composition is "divinely inspired in ordinariness" and uses utterly contextual, ahistorical language: "[n]one of the words Miss Stein uses have ever had any experience" (80). Most happily, Stein's work is unburdened by criticism and is conceived outside of the dreaded Zeitgeist: "This is how Gertrude Stein wrote in 1906 and this is how she was still writing in 1926. Writing by always beginning again and again and again keeps everything different and everything the same" (83). For Riding, Stein radicalizes poetic language by refusing metaphysical complexity and by making the reader's primal encounter with language truly new. Thus the difficulty in reading Stein lies not in the words themselves, but in the ways they are rendered unfamiliar in the moment of the composition and in the act of reading. Stein exemplifies barbaric modernism by writing authentically as herself in the present, by creating a language-based poetry that lies at the very foundation of avant-garde poetics, even to the present day.

Out of these valuations of Stein's barbarism, *Contemporaries* sketches an alternative modernist project that works against, rather than with, the specialization and disciplinarity that had come to define poetic practice by the late 1920s. If modernists, as Riding extensively argues, accept and even accelerate modernity's gradual separation of the spheres of human knowledge and activity, a poetics of barbarism might return us to a state in which these activities and orientations had equal range: "In a barbaric society religion does not occupy one mental compartment, philosophy another, science another, painting another, poetry another, and so on. But religion is everything and everything is religion, philosophy is everything and everything is philosophy, and so on. In a civilized society, religion is a sentiment, philosophy a speculation, science a pursuit of knowledge, painting and poetry arts" (58). In a sense, Riding's desire to return to this barbaric state finds a close cousin in Eliot's description of the literary periods that predate the "dissociation of sensibility," in which poets "possessed a mechanism of sensibility which could devour any kind of experience" ("The Metaphysical Poets" 669). Yet the two differ—crucially for *Contemporaries*—in their responses to this shift in human experience. Eliot studies it, while Riding audaciously invites poets to overcome it, so that poetry "might be normal without being vulgar, and deal naturally with truth without being trite" or so that poetry might be "everything," and "everything" poetry (55).

After Contemporaries and Snobs

In the years following the publication of *Contemporaries*, Riding gradually distanced herself, both physically and philosophically, from the modernist debates she took on in the book. On the heels of *Contemporaries*, she wrote *Anarchism is Not Enough*, a text written in response to Wyndham Lewis's *The Art of Being Ruled* (1926), which derided the "picturesque dementia of Gertrude Stein" and her "childish" cohort (416). After Riding's suicide attempt in 1929 (the impetus for which remains the subject of great debate), she and Graves relocated to Mallorca and lived there in relative isolation until the impending Spanish Civil War forced them to flee. During Riding's convalescence, Stein ceased to communicate with her, and after several of Riding's letters went unanswered, their friendship ended in 1930. In the years leading up to the Second World War, the problem of professionalism descried in *Contemporaries* and the importance of the modernist project more generally were eclipsed by the increasingly sinister geopolitical landscape and by Riding's own growing frustration with abstract language and metaphor. During this period, she drafted an "Open Letter" to hundreds of writers and artists asking "What shall we do?" about the rise of fascism; she wrote *Everybody's Letters*, a semi-fictional compendium of her correspondence from various friends and writers, and *The Word 'Woman,'* which investigates gender, language, and the ambivalent muse (and is almost certainly a reflection on her relationship with Graves). In 1938, Riding published her *Collected Poems*, after which she publicly repudiated poetry and ceased to write it. As Charles Bernstein has noted, Riding, like many public intellectuals in the midst of war, experienced a "crisis of and for expression, in which the abuse of language became inextricably identified with the abuse of the human" (259). Leaving Europe (and Graves) behind by 1940, Riding relocated to New York and married journalist Schuyler Jackson, changing her name (for the final time) to Laura (Riding) Jackson, with intentional parentheses. Increasingly reclusive in her writing and personal life, she and Jackson moved to rural Florida and adopted an ascetic lifestyle—living in a cabin with no electricity or running water, cultivating oranges, and writing together a *Dictionary of Related Meanings*. After Jackson's death in 1968, Riding continued to work on the *Dictionary*, which went through several iterations, and eventually became a lengthy philosophical treatise on language itself that was published posthumously as *Rational Meaning: A New Foundation for the Definition of Words* (1997).

Completely severed from those "contemporaries and snobs" she analyzed in the 1920s, Riding achieved in her later writing—especially *The Telling* and *Rational Meaning*—the idiosyncrasy that even her peripheral involvement in modernism never fully allowed. Reflecting on those years in "The New Immorality," she explains: "I have, thus, been given the role, in the historical drama Twentieth-Century Literature, of a non-belonger, one resisting the camaraderie of spoken-word literary linguisticism—and accorded the shabby honor of being dubbed 'neglected' by specialists in obscurities of literary justice. *And* I have deemed it my duty to bear myself, against that role-assignment, as the true belonger—were there a contemporary actuality of literature as the home of the written word (the word of purposeful thought) to which to belong" (261). Despite Riding's sense of her own isolation—that she belonged in a canon of one—and despite the increasingly arch, even mystical tone she adopted in her later work, the long view of modernism Riding outlines in *Contemporaries* inaugurates its own significant tradition. Whether or not she would welcome the associations, *Contemporaries* prefigures later feminist critiques of male modernism, as well as Marxist understandings of criticism and its effect on literature as a discipline. Above all, *Contemporaries* gives critical shape to an avant-garde tradition with Stein as its figurehead—a genealogy of poets who value and uphold the eccentricities of poetry, the particularity of the poet, and the true difficulty of human language. We cannot underestimate, then, the value of Riding's treatise in the history of modernist criticism, nor the value of her outsider perspective on modernism. Neither contemporary nor snob, she was uniquely situated to recognize its radicality as well as its weaknesses. In view of both, it is Riding's instinctive defense of the poet as person and of the inherent idiosyncrasy of the poetic endeavor that distinguishes *Contemporaries* and asks us to revisit and reevaluate the modernist enterprise.

Works Cited

Anonymous. "*Contemporaries and Snobs* by Laura Riding." *Times Literary Supplement*, April 5, 1928, 254.

Bernstein, Charles. "Riding's Reason." In *My Way: Speeches and Poems*, 255–267. Chicago: University of Chicago Press, 1999.

Eliot, T. S. "Charleston, Hey! Hey!" *Nation & Aethenaeum*. January 1927, 595.

———. "The Metaphysical Poets." *Times Literary Supplement*, October 20, 1921, 669.

———. *The Sacred Wood: Essays on Poetry and Criticism*. London: Methuen, 1960. First published 1920.

Friedmann, Elizabeth. *A Mannered Grace: The Life of Laura Riding Jackson*. New York: Persea, 2005.

Graves, Robert, and Laura Riding. *A Survey of Modernist Poetry*. London: William Heinemann, 1927.

Jackson, Laura (Riding). "An Autobiographical Summary." Laura (Riding) Jackson and Schuyler B. Jackson collection, #4608. Division of Rare and Manuscript Collections, Cornell University Library, n.d., series 1, box 1, folder 1.

———. "The New Immorality." In *Under the Mind's Watch: Concerning Issues of Language, Literature, Life of Contemporary Bearing*. Edited by John Nolan and Alan J. Clark. Bern, Switzerland: Peter Lang, 2004, 241–259.

Lewis, Wyndham. *The Art of Being Ruled*. London: Chatto and Windus, 1926.

McGann, Jerome. "The Grand Heretics of Modern Fiction: Laura Riding, John Cowper Powys, and the Subjective Correlative." *Modernism/modernity* 13, no. 2, (2006): 309–323.

Riding, Laura. *Contemporaries and Snobs*. New York: Doubleday Doran & Company, 1928.

———. "The New Barbarism and Gertrude Stein." *transition* 3 (June 1927): 153–68.

———. to Wyndham Lewis, April 22, 1927. Wyndham Lewis collection, #4612. Division of Rare and Manuscript Collections, Cornell University Library, box 112, folder 97.

———. *See also Jackson, Laura (Riding).*

Samuels, Lisa. "Creating Criticism: An Introduction to *Anarchism Is Not Enough.*" *Anarchism Is Not Enough* by Laura Riding. Berkeley: University of California Press, 2001, xi–lxxviii.

Stein, Gertrude. "Composition as Explanation." In *A Stein Reader*, edited by Ulla Dydo. Evanston: Northwestern University Press, 1993, 493–503.

———. *Three Lives and Tender Buttons*. New York: Signet Classics, 2003.

West, Geoffrey. *Deucalion: Or the Future of Literary Criticism*. London: Kegan Paul, Trench, Trubner, 1930.

Wexler, Joyce. "Epilogue: How Modernist Authority Became Authoritarian." In *Little Magazines and Modernism: New Approaches*, edited by Adam McKible and Suzanne W. Churchill. London: Ashgate, 2007, 133–147.

CONTEMPORARIES
and
SNOBS

1
Poetry and the Literary Universe

I: Shame of the Person

There is a sense of life so real that it becomes the sense of something more real than life. Spatial and temporal sequences can only partially express it. It introduces a principle of selection into the undifferentiating quantitative appetite and thus changes accidental emotional forms into deliberate intellectual forms; animal experiences related by time and space into human experiences related in infinite degrees of kind. It is the meaning at work in what has no meaning; it is, at its clearest, poetry.[1]

Unfortunately this sense, which can in its origin be only a *personal* one, is easily professionalized. From observations of it in written works, rules are made for it, intentions ascribed to it. There results what has come to be called criticism. Criticism in turn uses this sense against itself. It dissociates it from its creative origin. In the end the "literary" sense comes to be the authority-to-write which the poet is supposed to receive, through criticism, from the age that he lives in. It is not even in each age a new literary sense, but merely a tradition revised and brought up to date. More and more the poet has been made to conform to literature instead of literature to the poet—literature being the name given by criticism to works inspired by or obedient to criticism. Less and less is the poet permitted to rely on personal authority. The very word *genius*, formerly used to denote the power to intensify a sense of life into a sense of literature, has been boycotted by criticism; not so much because it has become gross and meaningless through sentimentality as because professional literature develops a shame of the person, a snobbism against the personal self-reliance which is the nature of genius. What is all current literary modernism but the will to extract the literary sense of the age from the Zeitgeist at any cost to creative independence? The readiness to resort to any contemporary fetish rather than to the poetic person? To strengthen its argument this snobbism may use all the unfortunate examples in poetry of reliance on the person: they are the moral lesson to which it does not even need to point. The fortunate examples it does not explain as reliance on the person but as authorized literature.

It was not until the late sixteenth century that the literary sense began to be professionalized in English literature, and then only loosely. The Elizabethan literary sense was capricious and eccentric. It contradicted itself. It was a grotesque but charming combination of coarse exuberance and elaborate refinement. There are uniform eccentricities in Elizabethan poetry because Elizabethan poets were personally alive in an eccentric age, not because, as a mass, they obeyed a contemporary programme. A constant human character runs through all the literature of this period, accentuated by the active share that most of the writers took in public life, which must be distinguished from the constant *literary* character of eighteenth-century literature, most of whose writers were also active in public life, but in a public life standardized in party politics. And although Elizabethan literature had a certain conformity of manner, it had little conformity of structure. It is impossible to treat any of the prevailing literary habits as items in a contemporary corpus. Euphuism, the luxurious politico-allegorical conceits of Spenser, the Arcadian refinements of Sidney, the pastoral affectations of Lodge, Peele and Greene, the philosophical realism of Shakespeare, even the foreign fashions reborrowed after Chaucer from the French and the Italian Renaissance—all of these were the erratic creative gestures of a time of erratic personality.

The period following the post-Elizabethan decay and the Puritan usurpation (roughly covering the first three-quarters of the eighteenth century) pulled itself together with French classicism. It wished to wipe out Elizabethan irregularity and its consequences. It looked down upon the Elizabethans because they had been too much alive. Said Johnson of Shakespeare: "A minute analysis of life at once destroys that splendour which dazzles the imagination; whatsoever grandeur can display or luxury can enjoy, is procured by offices of which the mind shrinks from contemplation." It is natural that this shrinking mind should have found its happiest expression in a form as negative as satire.

For between these two periods there was born the natural man, the commonsense antithesis to the erratic person. He was now in the centre of the stage and on all fours. Serving as a literary and sociological convenience, he did not act originally; he did not act at all. It was his function to be observed. "The proper study of mankind is man." Conduct in the abstract now became, in the hands of these early behaviourists, the morbid final value of the cultivated mind. The sole provision left the creative genius was an impersonal intelligence which, not guided by feelings, had to be guided by good manners.

Donne, an advanced contemporary of Shakespeare's, stands like a Janus between these two periods, in a separate period of his own, however—"to himself a Diocletian." On the one hand, he had more intellectual reserve than the Elizabethans; his poetry did not prove enduringly popular, as so much Elizabethan poetry did, because the proportion of surface-entertainment in it was smaller. On the other hand, his satiric epistles have a lyrical flexibility generally foreign to satiric poetry. The strength of the satires of Dryden, or, after him, Pope, lies in an energetic critical obedience, a contemporary piety, we might say; of Donne, in a sturdy and unruly self-reliance. The eighteenth-century satire was a literary custom, the least human and experimental form possible; while in Donne the satire was a vehicle of strong humanity and daring. Eighteenth-century literary policy demanded a formal inhumanity of the poet, since humanity was according to contemporary belief merely a philosophical abstraction upon which to moralize. Instead of passion, there was intelligence; and intelligence meant a servility to certain canonical ideas according to which the learning of the time was framed. Poets became, in the satire, ministers of instruction. By philosophy the poet was conceived and by classicism he had grace.

But what was philosophy more than the callow sophistries of deism or optimism or perfectionism? And what was classicism more than a plausible gloss to sophistries that could not without verbal pompousness support their inconsistencies? The poet was not a person but the spokesman of his age, a mechanical recorder of time. But time is only criticism and a poet is supposed to have to do with poetry. Poetry is not contemporary poetry. It is not philosophy. It is not even literature. As between literature and life, it is closer to life. But life invents time rather than poetry, a sanctimonious comment on itself, a selflessness. Poetry invents itself. It is nearly a repudiation of life, a selfness. Unless it is this, it is a comment on a comment, sterile scholasticism.

Public interference with poetry rests on the popular delusion that an immediate commerce exists between historical truth and poetic truth; that the historical universe is potentially the poetic universe. The historical universe is, however, only a temporary aggregate of ideas. These ideas may direct the structure of the literary universe, which produces the philosophical journalism of a period; the structure of the poetic universe is directed by a person in single-handed conflict with the time-community. Science, the present-day aggregate of tribal ideas, puts on the creative mind a social compulsion to accept these ideas; and criticism acts, as usual, as the nattered instrument of conversion. Official literature is born of a critical rather than of a literary sense; it is a social institution which the poet is hired to serve.

Criticism makes time-poets, who court favour for literature from the historical universe. A great deal of up-to-date poetry is thus written which becomes immediately out-of-date and is therefore rejected by the criticism that called for it; which consoles itself with a cynical classicism, a cult-cult of previous exemplary time-poets (such as Pope). The truth is that critical modernism is really more interested in maintaining a defensive attitude toward the literary past than in sponsoring "new" poetry. It equivocates between an unreserved adherence to poetic formalism and an unreserved disavowal of poetic formalism. It outformalizes formalism and thus has a ready snobbism to employ against formalism or irregularity, as may be required. Any new poetry which finds it necessary to disconnect itself from previous poetry, as Rimbaud's did, must be written outside the shelter of contemporary criticism of any sort; its creator must be "le grand malade, le grand criminel, le grand maudit—et le suprême savant. Car il arrive à l'inconnu."[2] Even the most advanced phase of critical modernism is in many respects more reactionary than the most conservative phase of contemporary critical traditionalism. For the latter, in its greybeard innocence, is sentimentally inclined toward any new idea that can be socially administered and justified personally on inspirational grounds: it has a pious hunger for the unknown and a superstitious respect for prophecy. The former, on the contrary, has an intellectual distaste for the unknown and an abhorrence of personal exhibitionism: shame in the person, as found in the various inhibitions which govern critical modernism, is the real reason for abetting the known historical universe. Even the element of obscurity resulting from an observance of the official shame-taboo is strictly limited to an obscurity of reference.

The presence of excessive criticism in a time is a sign that it fears its own literature; and overzealous critics are the agents of a compromise between poetry and society. They keep peace by forcing poetry to hide its personal criminalities behind the privilege-walls of literary tradition; they apply pressure only to poetry in the making, never to society. The gospel of contemporaneity is an expression of the mob-fear of the organized society of time against those incorruptible individuals who might reveal life to be an anarchy whose only order is a blind persistence. In the energy of this persistence occur intense flashes, the poetry or lightning of sense. The mob, looking on, reads an official code of revelation. Otherwise it must admit the mind of man to dwell in man; which would be as troublesome as fire in the brain and as shameful as thunder in the stomach.

II: Poetry, Out of Employment, Writes on Unemployment

The social office of poetry in both classical and romantical periods has been to formulate progress. It has been called upon to do this because history, philosophy, religion, science, even literature itself in so far as it is a knowledge-category, are constantly changing forms of wisdom that need the language of finality to help them impose themselves as absolute upon their periods. So it is that human tyrannies have enlisted poetry to conceal their insufficiencies, at the same time denying to poetry its own self-sufficiency. It was against such tyrannies that Shelley rebelled. But though he felt the social subjection of poetry more intensely than any poet before him, he attempted to justify its independence by its social excellence.

For while poetry was "at once the centre and circumference of knowledge, which comprehends all science and to which all science must be referred,"[3] it had also a civic usefulness ("The production and assurance of pleasure in this highest sense is true utility") since "the great instrument of moral good is the imagination; and poetry administers to the effect by acting as the cause." Poetry still remained, even in Shelley's view, a first-rate public servant jealous of its duties. He could go so far as to prove the superiority of poetry to other forms of human wisdom in its benefits to society; he could not go so far as to dissociate the critical from the social values of poetry, because he still thought of poetry as communal poetry, of the poet in his primitive function as the community's all-round medicine-man and of society as the origin of poetry through the action and interaction of the social sympathies. Indeed he seems to be defending poetry not so much for its own as for society's sake and thus translating his poetic incorruptibility into social orthodoxy instead of into real criticism. Much of the criticism and much of the poetry he wrote was only earnest propaganda for goodness.

This common misapplication of poetry to supplementary offices is the result of a confusion between an intelligence that we may call concrete, because it regards everything as potentially comprehensible and measurable, and the poetic intelligence, which is an accurate sensation of the unknown, an inspired comprehension of the unknowable. The concrete intelligence suffers from the illusion of knowledge since it does not recognize a degree in knowledge at which all its laws and implements cease to operate and at which another order of intelligence enters. It is at this degree that the poetic intelligence begins, an illuminating ignorance in which everything is more than certain, that is, absolute because purely problematical. The degree, which is one of clarity, is presupposed in the poet, whatever the condition of knowledge may be at his time, however far knowledge may be from the knowledge-limit. The poetic intelligence is a fixed proportion, the concrete intelligence a relative one. Confusion of these has led to the establishment of false rational equivalents to the poetic intelligence: so that, as in the present time, when the illusion of knowledge seems completely to satisfy the vanity of the concrete intelligence, poetry becomes a superfluous office and is either peremptorily dismissed or allowed to continue as a graceful tribute to the triumph of the concrete intelligence. However, the dignity historically conferred by society on poetry for its prophetic usefulness makes it impossible for poetry to accept this humiliation. (To use Shelley's distinction, society was using prophecy in the gross sense of the word, in which poetry was an attribute of prophecy, while poetry applied to this public charge the most favourable interpretation possible, in which prophecy was an attribute of poetry.) A competition ensues between the concrete intelligence and the poetic intelligence, futile because it cannot produce an increase in knowledge and because it has the effect on the poet of a snobbish display of contemporary sophistication. Indeed, in an actual hand-to-hand conflict between these two intelligences, the concrete intelligence would necessarily occupy the defensive position, since it takes only a very small pressure from the unknown to overthrow the most quantitatively formidable known. As a matter of fact no such practical contact can exist between them. For though one begins where the other leaves off, they are separated by the very degree which marks the change from one kind into another. Even if it were possible for the concrete intelligence to arrive at the full knowledge-limit, it would not automatically pass into the next stage but have achieved self-destruction and exhaustion; and the poetic intelligence would continue irrespective of accidents to the concrete intelligence, it being not a consumable surplus of intellectual power but a constant surplus. The relation between these two kinds of intelligence is further falsified by making the poetic intelligence the internal consciousness of the external concrete intelligence; whereas both have a strictly separate set of internal and external experiences, the external experience of the poetic intelligence being the personal life of the poet, the internal experience of the concrete intelligence being the impersonal mechanical soul which facts in a certain stage of assimilation assume and which gives to them a false poetic appearance of significant unity. Poets sin most of all perhaps in identifying this mass-consciousness, which contemporaneous facts seem to form automatically, with the self-consciousness of the poetic intelligence. (Paul Valéry is an exaggerated contemporary instance of this weakness. He made a gigantic effort to accomplish poetically the synthesis of the various modern knowledge-forms of the concrete intelligence and got, not a poetic equivalent, but a mathematical sum, a mystical number not further translatable into poetry. Having thus brought the concrete intelligence and the poetic intelligence of the present time to a deadlock and exerted a damping influence on creative enthusiasm, he was obliged to write his own poetry in the past to remove it from the necessity of accounting for itself otherwise than technically.)

The nineteenth century showed a more material increase than perhaps any other preceding century in this mass-consciousness of human knowledge which had for so long been feeding on poetry while pretending to feed it. There was a chance that, dismissed from pseudo-poetic occupations, poetry might enter into its proper domain. But the old connection was too strong a literary habit and poetry continued to search for a poetic equivalent to the newly enlarged universe long after this universe, so increasingly intelligible to itself, had begun to deny the reality of poetic values (as it was right in doing if poetic values are understood as interpretative values). As an epic is the most tangible poetic equivalent to a group of associated rational experiences, poets went on writing in an epic vein, but without producing an epic, since normally an epic cannot be produced without a historical demand for it—the nineteenth century was finding its own epic in progressive material expansion. The character put upon this futile Victorian type was *realism*, to describe the rational tests to which poetry submitted itself and which therefore made it slavish and petty in substance, in manner disproportionately grandiose. Tennyson's *Princess* and other similar writings designed to make poetry keep pace with progress never looked anything but feeble and old-fashioned beside progress itself.

With the advance of the twentieth century, *progress* was gradually dropped from the vocabulary of the concrete intelligence as too small a word for so large a thing; and *relativity* permitted to take its place, not for its mathematical sense, but because it was the most poetic word available in scientific language to convey the immensity of the great atomic epic of the concrete intelligence.[4] Poetry, as the diminutive prophet of progress, was also dropped out. Even history, the life-size image of man, made a philosophical recantation of faith in the personal mind, and a new century had its moment when it declared formally that the myth of humanity was no more. This meant a complete isolation of the poetic intelligence in the personal unknown, in an unconquerable interior: a state that had been the unconscious desire of poetry since its beginnings as a community handmaiden of tribal success, that is, of progress. The liberation of the poetic intelligence from its indenture would coincide, naturally, with the disappearance of poetry as such in the social sense of the word. Poetry had become the property of society and like any other manufactured commodity had ceased to have any organic connection with its makers. It might now be possible to re-establish this connection.

It was to be hoped that criticism would use its offices to bring this about. But as criticism's professional status depended on the maintenance of the old order, it could not be expected to celebrate poetry's forced dissociation from social uses. The best it could do was to believe cheerfully that nothing had really changed and protest against poetry's exclusion from social uses. It could insist upon looking for the joke. The joke was found. The universe still had a myth requiring the ritualistic services of poetry. The new myth was that there was no myth. Delighted with this discovery, criticism rushed to the rescue of the unnumbered poets who, being individuals and not, like criticism, a public institution, had perhaps not noticed that anything was happening at all but continued to write as they had always written, for reasons that they left to others to discover. For people never really live in contemporary history: they live either in the past or completely outside the time-sense. So the course of criticism (or of certain forces and influences which, by their effect, become criticism) was to announce, first, that historical conditions had put an end to poetry, removing all hope in order to bring home to poets the proper time-sense, then, to follow this melancholy report with the cheerful amendment that, after all, all hope was not gone, since, if poetry had all subjects taken away from it, there was always one subject of which poetry could not be deprived, namely, that poetry had come to an end. Here was an ingenious method for indefinitely postponing the end of poetry; and, after the general applause which followed this remarkable solution, many volunteers stepped forward and declared feelingly that the time-sense had been brought home to them and that, now that it had been made clear to them that poetry was at an end, they felt sure that they could write better poetry than ever. Never indeed, they said, had such an urgent reason for writing poetry been presented to poets. Under the spell of this enthusiasm a tremendous revival of poetry took place; and not only was better poetry, but more poetry than ever written. Since poetry was to write about nothing, it could write about everything from the standpoint of nothing; it could still have its epic without the burden of having to have convictions about it.

The most notable exponent of this non-committal epic was T. S. Eliot. His period poem fulfilled the time-sense requirements even to the point of self-extinction. It was indeed everything and nothing. It composed and decomposed. It was contemporaneously sympathetic and contemporaneously apathetic. It ran from classical minor to romantic major, to romantic minor, to classical major and back again. It disciplined itself learnedly in the pious unbelief of scholasticism. Everything is Nothing. But Nothing is eternal. "We have not reached conclusion. . . ."[5]

Unreal City,
Under the brown fog. . . .
Falling towers
Jerusalem Athens Alexandria
Vienna London
Unreal[6]

One would have thought this left nothing to be desired. But one thing had been overlooked in this revival, the importance of not being earnest. Poetry had perhaps taken the time-sense too literally, had been too much of an advocate and therefore too little of a snob against itself: even irony can betray convictions if it becomes too ironical. Or, to put the complaint practically, this posthumous poetry was not formal enough: it bore too little resemblance to poetry proper. This was the general objection made by many who were on the inside, so to speak, of the movement to keep poetry going. Mr. Edwin Muir is a typical spokesman of the reaction against intensity.[7] T. S. Eliot, he protests in effect, is a true posthumist, but too heartbreaking. Edith Sitwell is also a true posthumist and has, besides, a strict technical organization of her non-humanistic universe of death-in-life. She has, in fact, managed to leave the heart-break out. But even this does not satisfy Mr. Muir, to whom such a complete extinction of the heart-break seems to bespeak a stoicism likely to become, in its own way, paradoxically intense; so that he begs Miss Sitwell to reinstate the heart-break. Nor does Robert Graves satisfy in any respect, since he is too casual, and so not a posthumist at all. Because he constantly changes (as he makes personal rather than critical interpretation of the time-sense) he is, Mr. Muir concludes, creatively unbalanced; that is, he disregards the official demise of the poetic intelligence and writes on a realistic basis, making private terms with the time-sense instead of negotiating with it through critical headquarters. (This desire to look for secret understandings in Mr. Graves' poetry has led Mr. Muir to morbid misinterpretations of certain of his poems, such as *The Clipped Stater*, in which Mr. Muir reads only as a flirting with the theory of metempsychosis what is a poetic narration of the personal absolute, dramatized as the deified Alexander the Great, experimenting with the time and space humiliations of historical life.)

To illustrate just what he considers to be the proper tone for posthumist poetry, Mr. Muir has gone to the trouble of writing a little specimen poem to be used, perhaps, as the standard posthumistic primer and very fittingly named, indeed, *Chorus of the Newly Dead*. A single stanza will serve to show what Mr. Muir means. The Poet says:

And through our souls the vast tormented world
Passed slow in splendid pictures without pain.
Where, in what distant night, have these been hurled?
When shall dawn rise on those lost mounts again?

As this method seems to be no more than the adoption of the Tennysonian hat, mantle and trousers with Tennyson left out, posthumistic poets should not find it difficult to follow, especially since such minute instructions for the playing of the part are contained in T. S. Eliot's *Hollow Men*.

The throw-back to the ordinary poetic tradition in which the fanatic observance of the contemporary time-sense has culminated reminds us that this time-sense is nothing but the familiar historical Zeitgeist in a more complicated disguise than usual. It would be well to recall here the distinction between the formal Zeitgeist, as it is manifested in literature—in contemporary poetry for example—and the personal literary sense, as it was possessed by the Elizabethans. The former translates a whole period into a single emotion which is used as artificial colouring for the period's literature. The latter is the actual, the moving nerve of many emotions, which do not need to have existed as worn-out history before they can enter poetry: they are historical only in the sense that they may compose poetry—but not historical until the poetry is composed. Zeitgeist poetry is out-of-date poetry, because it describes an emotion derived from history. A faithful, up-to-date historical record of this emotion may be inspired by the Zeitgeist, but not an up-to-date poetry; for the poetry it purposes to inspire was or was not written in the time when the period was a period, before it was called a period. All Zeitgeist poetry is, in truth, posthumous poetry; and it is periods of poetry that die, because periods die, not poetry. Byron, Goethe and Lamartine, for example, who considered themselves poetic universalists, were typical Zeitgeist writers, much more important as the recording spirits of a period of revolution and reaction which they helped to bury, than as poets: their poetry died as it was being written. There is a way of living in history that goes forward, but by facing backwards; and poetry written in this way cannot claim to belong anywhere.

III: Escapes from the Zeitgeist

Satire

A certain amount of poetic activity naturally seeks to protect itself from the Zeitgeist by making use of one of two historically respectable modes—the nature-mode or the satire-mode; or, disdaining these, it may retire to the proud exile of what is known as the poetic absolute. With the coming of age of the universe the infant call of nature is supposed to have been superseded by the vast silence of intelligence in matter (so that the poet has no more questions to answer, having lost his job as tutor in the nursery of time). The pathetic fallacy, however, still remains a possible romantic escape for sentiment in flight from a new system of facts; as irony, the antipathetic fallacy, for wit in flight from a new system of intellectual expediency.

Although the formal eighteenth-century satire was in some respects a romantic escape by classicism from threatening romanticism, it was more definitely an instrument of subjection to the Zeitgeist, one of literature's social mannerisms. Conforming satire must be distinguished from the satire of revolt, which is a weak gesture of social non-conformity. The former is the satire in its literal sense, an elegant and conscientious exercise in a form, a medley of localisms (the satire being by derivation a medley) on which stylistic uniformity is superimposed. When Dryden described wit as "the essence of all verse," he was using it in this satiric scissors-and-paste sense.[8] (It is interesting to notice that he did not say the essence of all *poetry*. Dryden is perhaps the founder of the snobbism, developed by eighteenth-century contempt of the person, which limits the use of *poetry* to great poetry, that is, bad poetry which succeeds in spite of itself. Before Dryden *verse* had been chiefly a poetical word; with Dryden it came to denote critical respectability. In the eighteenth century it was regularly applied to poetry too superior to be great poetry. *Verse* still prevails today, except in old-fashioned corners, as a term of deprecation which gratifies contemporary shame of the person and emphasizes the vulgarity of *poetry*.) Indeed Dryden was opposing practical wit to impassioned Elizabethan wit—"a finer speech than the language will allow," as it was defined for *Euphues or The Anatomy of Wit*.[9] Donne, it will be remembered, was abused by Johnson because he had employed wit too earnestly. Speaking of Cowley, whom he considered superior to Donne, Johnson said: "The fault of Cowley, and perhaps of all writers of the metaphysical race, is that of pursuing his thoughts to their last ramifications, by which he loses the grandeur of generality."[10] Wit in the eighteenth century did not mean "happiness of language" (for which Johnson had to condemn even Pope) or happiness of thought, as it was for the metaphysicians.[11] It was the wit of the formal satire, a cozenage of contemporary banality called "strength of thought," the common sense of the prevailing system of intellectual expediency.

In the satire of revolt wit performs a philosophical evasion. It compromises with that which it opposes by treating it with a semi-playful, semi-sorrowful pessimism. Irony defeats sentiment, but in doing so it proves itself to be inverted sentiment, self-defeated. The most successful romantic satirist in contemporary poetry is John Crowe Ransom,[12] who by a happy conjunction of sentiment and irony, has managed to elevate defeat to a note of such unembittered renouncement that it amounts, in its suppressed optimism, to a dignified compromise with the all-conquering time-sense. This fortunate solution permits him to be a gentle and aristocratic non-conformer in his *métier* and a democrat in the adjustment of his poetry to its social *milieu*. A less astute satire of revolt is to be found in the poetry of Siegfried Sassoon. In his high-principled refusal of a helping hand from the Zeitgeist—a mixture of the fanatic and the debonair—he has a paradoxical bond with perhaps his most removed contemporary, James Joyce; who, by a colossal evasion, which involved swallowing the Zeitgeist and then vomiting it up again, accomplished the dual and monstrous feat of capitulation and revolt in one huge, involuntary reflex-spasm.

Satire in this non-conforming sense is obviously unfit to supply the period-poem which the age, through criticism, demands as its tribute from poetry. At its best it produces, like the conforming satire, period-tracts. The conforming eighteenth-century satire dissolved when its wit had exhausted its material, and the period-epic was driven into such obscurity as Darwin's *Botanic Garden*.[13] Only satire in a broad, summarizing sense may culminate in a representative epic, a large-scale poem of cancellation and substitution. And then it is generally accompanied by a prose morality which makes the work of cancellation easier. If however the age is in motion and yet lacking in constructive substitute values (whether specious or real) to replace disappearing values, the contemporary satire will probably be confined solely to the prose morality; it will be merely an epic of cancellation. Fielding was thus the real author of the eighteenth-century satiric epic. The nineteenth century was deficient in cancelling power and therefore produced no great contemporary satire. Like the eighteenth century, the present period can get no further than such an epic of cancellation as *Ulysses*; with the difference that, though both epics are equally devoid of creative values and alike designed to produce a catharsis of stale emotional matter (it is remarkable how closely the Fielding-epic and the Joyce-epic tally in material and structure—the use of obscenity, destructive literary criticism, minute reports of the working of the minds of plain people), the eighteenth-century view of literature made a place for the prose morality, while the ethics of contemporary criticism force the epic of cancellation to conclude with a cancellation of itself. Criticism is the voice of the age; and as the age feels itself the consciousness of an arrived universe, it does not call for an expression of new values or for a summary of the distribution of values, but merely for congratulation. The poetic consciousness, which criticism treats as a historical consciousness, has become superfluous. Poetry, however, will be permitted to indulge in the bravado of despair, the universe's mark of pity for poetry thus obliged to sever its connections with it. Poetry seeking to escape the Zeitgeist, and therefore not properly of this age, the universe leaves to an out-of-date criticism that seems to have survived by grace to take care of it. For poetry that is trying to win a postponement of judgment by good behaviour, the universe finds itself fortunately provided with an advanced criticism recruited largely from the ranks of poetry itself; so that the universe expects no trouble to come of its clemency—that is, it is not likely to have poets, though much poetry of an obituary nature. The important thing to be remembered by poetry is that shifting historical values have been brought to a state of equilibrium by the heavy forefinger of science and that there can therefore be no new values, only a methodic resolution of the values we have, which are, potentially at least, all the values there are: in life, if not in literature, we have reached conclusion. This is the lesson poetry is supposed to learn, and no more; lest, by meddling in science itself, it acquire the confidence of science and be tempted to observe that every age has had the illusion of an equilibrium and the illusion of new learning through revolutions in nomenclature.

The Poetic Absolute

The satire-escape and the nature-escape, creating as they do a moral barrier of protective contempt between the poet and the Zeitgeist, involve perhaps less equivocation than any other forms attempting to live in spite of the age.[14] A hypocritical and suppressed romanticism lurks in the resignation of professedly Zeitgeist poetry, a depression difficult at times to distinguish from self-pity. Not that there is anything wrong with romanticism in itself, but suppressed romanticism is pathological; which is why the only possible interpretation for much contemporary poetry is psycho-analytic. As the detachment in such poetry, of which *The Waste Land* is an easy clue for identification (and imitations of it like Nancy Cunard's *Parallax*), is not voluntary but forced on the poet by the universe from which he has been banished, its romanticism can be easily detected in its wasting, its loss of appetite and weight, its obvious pining for home. It is more difficult, however, to recognize suppressed romanticism in poetry which tries to achieve detachment by a pretentious creative system.

A great deal of literary shop-talk is devoted to the aesthetic absolute and a forced dignity attends any effort to free the poem from destructive circumstances which the poet is himself subject to. But there is a difference between that absoluteness in a poem which is the poet's own irrefutability, his power to write a poem that does not have to support him in his weakness, or be supported by him in its weakness; and that absoluteness which is philosophically read into a poem to give it an authority that the poet is unable to find in life. In the first sense absoluteness is a critical term that may be applied retrospectively to any good poem. In the second it is a moralistic-philosophical term to be applied *prospectively* to the compensating function the poem is supposed to perform in the poet's and everybody's life. Not until this distinction is perceived do we become aware of the romantic unfulfilment and disappointment which most theories of the absolute conceal.

The imposition of an absolute on the poem means the exclusion of all loose relative references, the use of symbols that have no association outside of the literary range of the poem itself, and an effect of great technical rigidity that we may call creative strain. Hart Crane is perhaps the only contemporary romantic absolutist who succeeds in matching technical tenseness with emotional tenseness.[15] He maintains the ideal of romantic absoluteness by admitting the philosophical dualism on which it is really based: he postulates a normal and an abnormal reality, and his poems are real in so far as they identify one reality with the other. In this he is an exception to the usual romantic absolutist whose poems achieve a fixed mechanical reality by excluding all correspondences—they are real because they admit no reality but their own. Rimbaud, the last-century absolutist most relied on by contemporary absolutists, made intellectual monstrosity the first condition of poetic finality—an "immense et raisonné dérèglement de tous les sens."[16] But in him intellectual monstrosity was a personal fact rather than a poetic theory, one so intensified by poetic abuse that he was obliged, in the end, to turn normal, to suppress his personal monstrosity in order to avoid destruction through creative strain.

Evidences of creative strain in contemporary poets who profess no theory of the absolute reveal the same effort to escape from the destructive influences of the Zeitgeist into the constructive possibilities of the poem when viewed as totality. In virtue of his creative strain E. E. Cummings may be considered effectively an absolutist. His technical caprice is a deliberate dissociation from contemporary reason. (He is generally labelled an impressionist; but this only means that he treats his absolute, his poem, as a stage-joke, and that humour introduces sympathy, memory and related experience. His absolute may be more properly called the comic relief of the absolute.) In Marianne Moore, from whom all thoughts of the absolute must be far removed, creative strain is a conscientious, scientific analysis of the germs which are assumed to be responsible for the poetic condition; and her absolute is that pure residuum of mental activity which is left when the imagination has been excluded and, with it, sympathetic affiliations with emotional environment. Edith Sitwell's absolute is perhaps more perplexing than any of these. For though the technical pattern is maintained by strain, the strain itself proves to be merely the romantic inventiveness of frankly trivial emotions. But it would be absurd to deny that Miss Sitwell's poetry had an absolute simply because it was romantic, that is, because it confessed the triviality of escape. It is this refreshing and disarming frankness which makes her work so popular. Her absolute seems all the more genuine because, besides being fixed, formalized romance, it is also an imitation of the practical absolute of modern pictorial art. The absolute of painting is a technical necessity imposed by the limitations of the medium. It may therefore develop into a mature creative fact in painting, while in poetry, except where the methods of painting are deliberately imitated, it rarely goes beyond the stunt stage. Since Miss Sitwell arbitrarily adopts the methods of painting, her poetry passes beyond the stunt stage. Yet it is not quite fair to say that it is poetry written with the methods of painting, for this would mean that it was something neither poetry nor painting. Miss Sitwell, by the careful use of a limited number of symbols (of constant value and fairly uniform recurrence), actually creates paintings, not poems; which, from the inferred poetic value of these symbols, may be made into poems by the reader. By confining herself to painting (which is her real medium) in poetry, she succeeds in writing poetry and in immortalizing it in picture-frames labelled *romantic*. Inside the picture-frame everything is, as has so often been pointed out, motionless. But the label reminds one that the painted cherry is able to hang so still only because it is painted.

The safest form of poetic absolute is probably one derived from a theological absolute. In France—where poetry has a great tendency to let itself be written by the Zeitgeist; where the poet is supposed to be the man of numbers who is sensible, in the words of Paul Valéry, the present high-priest of Zeitgeist mysticism, of the *passage de l'infinité des individus*;[17] and where national vanity makes poetry an opportunistic blend of the romantic and the classical, of accidental crowd literature and academic *grand homme* literature — Catholicism provides a practical refuge in which the poet can write with creative purity. Absolutes must go in pairs, one the assumption, the other the demonstration; and when the assumption on which the poetic absolute is based is vaguely formulated, as it is likely to be if a critical assumption, the poem gives an effect of insincerity and false power. The principle of technical dissociation from influences, on which the absolute poem is supposed to depend, best follows from such an article of faith as Jean Cocteau expresses uncritically in: "J'apprendrai à *fabriquer* les poèmes (le mot est de La Fontaine) et pour le reste à laisser faire Dieu."[18] If the absolute poem is, as the professed absolutist pretends, a superior experience, then it can have no value as superior experience unless it is accompanied by an expressed belief in the possibility of a superior experience: the poetic absolute at its most literal implies religious experience. A child is the perfect absolutist, since by an initial acquiescence of the imagination in everything, it makes the general one absolute, the particular another. The result is an independence of the particular from the general, though it suggests the general as one complementary colour suggests another: a quality for which simplicity is perhaps a happier term than absoluteness. The want of simplicity is the striking discrepancy in most "absolute" poetry and poetic theory.

An absolute confers freedom in return for recognition, and freedom should confer health, clearness, courage and variety. What is our contemporary absolute poetry like?—*Health?* It is ashen with misanthropy—*Clearness?* Where technical intricateness permits any light to shine through, it is a light thinned out by a mystical vanity in defeat. An absolute implies fulfilment; and mysticism is a simple instrument of success. Indeed, a poetry that takes its absolute from a religious absolute does not have to trouble to be either mystical or religious; it does not have to confound its own intensity with argument. The non-religious romantic absolute in poetry, having no supporting absolute, is obliged to be overcharged with sophistication.—*Courage?* How may such an evasive dogmatism presume to make attacks on open, intrenched dogmatisms? On science? On literature itself? "Imaginez, mon cher Jacques, la joie d'une langue dégagée de Rimbaud (à l'heure actuelle plus encombrant que Hugo) et de la superstition de Maldoror. La jeunesse respirerait."[19*] We gasp for the air in which to make declarations of similar freedom. Our most uncompromising poetic programme is a string of fine names (Donne, Poe, Rimbaud) worn as a charm round the neck of the snob-aesthete.—*Variety?* The only material sign of absoluteness in so-called absolute poetry is a technical limit the approach to which means an increasing effect of monotony: the absolutist is only interesting in his lapses.

What is here concealed? A timid desire or a perverse will to write poetry which shall not involve personal accountability; disguised as a protective snobbism against the Zeitgeist, which is seen as vulgarity sitting in moral judgment. But if the poem is to be protected from moral judgments it must have a morality of its own; and the morality of a poem cannot reside in mere technical integrity. Technical integrity should presuppose a scrupulous respect between the poet and the poem, and this cannot exist if the poem is a convenience of the poet, a kind of moral dummy. It is then but an annex

* Jean Cocteau, "Lettre à Jacques Maritain."—Author

of the poet, and without morality, as the poet, being without morality, becomes an instrumental annex of the poem. The poem cannot be absolute unless it belongs to itself; and it cannot belong to itself unless the poet belongs to himself. The poet, then, is the true companion absolute of the poetic absolute, which in this light acquires a simpler and more explicit critical character: it is the *goodness* of a poem without regard to its supplementary experience-value to the poet. But for a poem to be free of the necessity to provide experience-value the poet must have no poetic prejudice toward actual experience. He must not ask poetic truth of reality or realistic truth of poetry. He must see that there is logic but also illogic, "reality" but also an equally real or more real unreality. And he must be strong enough to endure in one person both kinds of experience. If the romantic absolute is the harmless invention of a personality strong enough to endure only one kind of experience, it is perhaps a legitimate device by which such a personality may have an illusion of power both in poetry and life. If, however, it threatens to impose as a doctrinaire metaphysic of poetry what is only a hypocritically and elegantly worded counsel of personal evasion, then it demands to be refuted by a complete rehabilitation of the poetic mind and by a bold reinstatement of the person in poetry. A rampant, undisguised romanticism is preferable to it, or an ingenuous religious profession.

This is the kind of extreme which the poetic intelligence may be driven to when the victorious concrete intelligence seems to have taken possession of all the facts of actual experience, leaving the poetic intelligence nothing but shadow with which to build a shadowy empire. It at first seems strange that the poetic intelligence should accept defeat so easily from the concrete intelligence. This is due, however, to the illusion of numbers which the concrete intelligence has always been able to practise. For it is, as has already been suggested, a mass-consciousness whose numerical index is a social unit rather than a personal one; a synthetic force, as the poetic intelligence is an analytic one, which at its weakest may disintegrate into its component groups (whose variety is a sign of its weakness, as the present inclusion of everything in one category, science, is a sign of its strength), such as the religious mind, the philosophical mind, the political mind, but never into individual units—when it reaches individual units it is the mass-consciousness once more. All arts except poetry are a cross between the concrete intelligence and the poetic intelligence: they have, by nature of their respective mediums, group rather than individual motivation. The poetic intelligence has therefore to fight alone against the aggressions of the concrete intelligence and, at times of intense synthesizing like the present, is even forced to disappear from itself or to cover its tracks with the dry leaves of philosophical sentiment. But for whom is poetry being advertised as possessing when read the virtue of an absolute? The concrete intelligence does not read, nor is reading done in dozens, or even in pairs. The only individual, then, whom it is safe to presume as a reader for poetry is the poet himself. But if he is obliged to advertise his poetry to himself, it is perhaps a sign that the poem is being asked to stand for a poetic intelligence wanting in the poet in proportion to the degree claimed for it in the poem: the poem is not self-determined, but merely the poet's personal implement of self-determination.

Another form of survival possible to the poetic intelligence, and one involving no definite break with the Zeitgeist (the family name of the concrete intelligence), is for it to submit itself to a test of physical endurance, that is, to produce a long poem. Contemporary efforts to make the poetic absolute consist in sheer structural impressiveness have been numerous. For example, Edith Sitwell's *Sleeping Beauty*, Aldous Huxley's *Leda*, W. J. Turner's *Paris and Helen*, John Masefield's *Reynard the Fox*, Alfred Noyes' *The Torchbearers*, Conrad Aiken's *Pilgrimage of Festus*, Roy Campbell's *The Flaming Terrapin*, V. Sackville-West's *The Land*, William Ellery Leonard's *Two Lives* or Edwin Arlington Robinson's *Tristram* can account for their length in no other way.

Nature

Of the various escapes from the Zeitgeist open to poetry the nature-escape offers the fewest obstacles. For, as to childhood, certain privileges are granted to the nature-feeling, chiefly the privilege of immaturity. Nature is that part of the universe which is at man's mercy and is spared by him so long as it acknowledges his lordship. Man's all-conquering mass-intelligence even permits nature to appear humanized, to make the drama between innocence and intelligence more vivid: nature is the world-as-universe's humorous indulgence of its own contemporaneous childhood. For this reason the nature-mode arouses less opposition in an environment hostile to poetry than other forms of romantic escape. But innocence, of which nature is the quaint symbol, presupposes that still quainter sophistication, irony. The irony of the nature-mode in a latter-day atmosphere is the mature handwriting in which innocence is written down; innocence cannot be put on record as such without an intellectual bias in its favour. The nature-mode avows intelligence even in forswearing intelligence: innocence is a conscious means of direct escape from the Zeitgeist or of demure flattery of it, of indirect escape.

The countryside element in late eighteenth-century poetry was inspired by the panic into which certain poets were thrown when they suddenly found poetry on its death-bed; they staggered to Nature's breast and, giving her a philosophicodeistic piece to speak, begged her to use all her eloquence to hold off the grim adversary. And though Goldsmith was "ignorant" and Collins, Gray and Cowper only slightly more "reasonable," Johnson never damned them completely. They gave the age an opportunity of justifying its intellectual refinements by comparison with a contemporaneous infancy—the nature of the countryside being the stupid foil to the intelligence of the coffee-house. The nature of twentieth-century poetry is the mouse which the lion spares to show how savage he really is.

But however demure and submissive the nature-mode may appear, it is, in its affected innocence, closer to active rebellion than any other form of poetic escape: it is capable at any moment of romantic controversy, of becoming the weapon of a new Zeitgeist against the old—a brief flush of triumph, then dissolution, even at the hands of the new Zeitgeist. Such, for instance, was the history of the late eighteenth-century nature-movement that took off from *Cooper's Hill* and ended in myth, far from home, among the Isles of Greece. It had had, or had seemed to have, the choice of connecting itself retrospectively with a formal uncontroversial nature-tradition or of converting nature into an imagination which would be able to overthrow the autocratic, adult regime of reason. In reality it had no choice but controversy. Close as was the *Cooper's Hill* tradition, Sir John Denham was but an isolated anachronism, a minor eighteenth-century nature-writer and moralist born a century too soon. Milton was the closest classical figure who might have constituted a literary inheritance, but his "nature" was a vulgar conglomeration of bookish references. Besides these, all else was dim, covered by the crooked shadow of the age of Pope. Pope himself made use of the nature-mode, like many of his contemporaries, as a formalistic reaction against the eccentric Elizabethan pastoral and its free personal use of the classical pastoral, as by Spenser, Fletcher and Browne; against the naturalness of the Elizabethan nature in general. In the hands of writers like Pope and Ambrose Philips the pastoral became an instrument of conformity with the Zeitgeist, a flattery of modernism: though Pope professed Virgil as his model and Philips, Spenser, the result was much the same in both. Their object was to stand *Cooper's Hill* between the eighteenth century and the barbaric Elizabethans, surmounted by the stern form of Milton (in the folds of whose robe were concealed so many of the gems he had taken from these barbarians because, presumably, they were too good for them). All that the literary past could furnish, therefore, to the storm about to break was provocation. *Cooper's Hill* may be regarded as the provocation to Keats' little hill of nonsense, as Milton may be regarded as the provocation to Blake's religious romanticism.

Militant romanticism is three parts defiance, one part constructive innovation. Begun as a reaction against prevailing literary snobbisms, it gives birth to new snobbisms, temporarily more tyrannical because they are emotional rather than intellectual snobbisms: that is, they do not merely conform to their Zeitgeist, they are part of it. It is therefore destructive of literary traditions, having to break down some to get at others which have been blocked—as Keats had to tear down two whole centuries to get at the Elizabethan pastoral-writers; but socially constructive, since the Zeitgeist is but a gigantic social movement; and so eventually a constructive literary influence. For while the actual productions of a romantic movement soon become absurd and lose literary significance, it, in turn, through its social modernism, makes a great many superannuated literary superstitions look absurd. The effect of the Industrial Revolution, for instance, on romanticism was not only to provide it with new subjects (literally so in the novel, as in *Shirley*, *Sybil* and *John Halifax, Gentleman*), but also to create a new *modern feeling* which the romantic movement helped to convey to literature. Early nineteenth-century political humanitarianism, again, had a more important influence on literature than the literary works of the romantic movement itself. It replaced eighteenth-century social definitions, which had existed in purely literary terms, with new social definitions in political terms and thus temporarily deprived literature, poetry in particular, of its social usefulness.

The amazing critical banalities of Wordsworth, the remote metaphysical propositions of Coleridge, the socio-political doctrines of Shelley are all part of an attempt to give poetry an eternal *poetic* usefulness. But the contemporary man still overshadowed the poet who only happened to be a contemporary man. The balance of influence was still with the Zeitgeist. The difference, however, between the characteristic eighteenth-century Zeitgeist and the characteristic early nineteenth-century Zeitgeist is that one was a dead weight around the neck of the poet, turning him into a literary drudge to society, the other a form of mass-hypnotism in which the poet had at least the illusion of freedom and voluntary participation in his time. Both were immoral; the latter, however, had the merit of allowing the poet to forget the mass-source of this hypnotism and to treat it as the first-hand inspiration of the poetic intelligence. The only difference that this made was, perhaps, in providing a less inhibited, if more foolish race of poets. Keats, for example, was far more inhibited than Shelley because he engaged consciously in literature and in literature alone. He would undoubtedly have been more comfortable in the eighteenth century: he was a better literary poet than Shelley (and than any other poet of his time); though not a better poet.

The application of this history to the contemporary problem of the nature-mode, to which it must return, may be slight. One thing appears certain, that the nature-mode is not threatening to break loose into militant romanticism.

It flashes upon us that we are not the twentieth century in the sense in which the eighteenth century, say, seemed to have been the eighteenth century; that upon the assumption of a coherent and peculiar Zeitgeist we have invented certain modes of escape from it, and certain modes of coming to terms with it; and that the only result is the increased vagueness of the Zeitgeist. Shall we give the nature-mode a push in order to have, some time soon, a romantic movement and a new modern feeling? Or shall we be classical in order to make the Zeitgeist talk more clearly?

Oh, Zeitgeist, had we but a Borrow or a Melville to apostrophize thee in the shameless manner of the 1840's! Thou art verily a sore weight and a millstone about our necks, and we have not offended the little ones. As a matter of fact, we are the little ones. Where art thou, Zeitgeist, that we may hang the millstone about thy neck and cast thee into the sea? The Zeitgeist is silent. Can it be possible that after all there *is* no Zeitgeist?

IV: Poetic Reality and Critical Unreality

The critical problem, then, is not so much a matter of the proper subjects or style-modes by which to ensure the integrity of poetry, as the determining of where the true reality of the poem lies, whether in the gross contemporary mind of which the poet is supposed to be possessed, or in the non-contemporary poetic mind—for poetic must mean non-contemporary if *contemporary* is understood as anything more than a historically descriptive phrase, if it is used, for example, to describe the mind as shaped by contemporary influences. If the distinction between these two minds is carefully drawn, it will be seen that, in times when the poetic mind has been under the dictatorship of the contemporary mind, the poem has had only contemporary reality; as in the eighteenth century, when the poem had a false poetic reality because the social dictatorship was disguised in the literary dictatorship, and as in the Victorian period, when the poem had a more obvious contemporary reality. In the early nineteenth century the poem had a mixed reality; the contemporary mind, in its caprice and inventiveness, imitating the poetic mind.

If we observe what happens when the poem is confined to one type of reality, to that of the contemporary mind, as in the eighteenth-century satire, or to that of the poetic mind, as in the romantic abuse of the poetic absolute, it appears that both of these are but half-realities and that the true reality of the poem must have a double force: a positive truth, from its origin in the poetic mind, and a negative truthfulness, from the fact that it is not made unreal when brought into contact with the contemporary mind, that is, with contemporary knowledge. When the contemporary mind, or the concrete intelligence, or whatever we please to call it, is seen to be no more, no less, than accumulated knowledge-material, it will be realized how grotesque it is that this should supply the creative origin, and hence the first reality of the poem, leaving to the poetic mind the secondary service of interpretation.

But the slaves of this knowledge-material can imagine no state of activity which shall not be dependent on it; they cannot understand that the poet can have experience of it as an independent mind reducing authoritative mass to unauthoritative ideas; that once the mass of intelligent matter is recognized as a mass of ideas about matter, every man is potentially his own scientist, though not his own poet, since only the poet is fully capable, in this way, of being his own scientist. Therefore, if the poet shows independence, if he is, indeed, not a mere mouthpiece of the contemporary mind, it is assumed by the knowledge-slaves that he cannot have an informed mind; and everything he writes is taken with a grain of scientific salt. This snobbism, which naturally appeals to criticism, because it seems another indulgence by which poetry may manage to survive, in turn drives poets who stand in fear of the knowledge-hierarchy to profess only the single reality of the poetic mind—what we may call the apologetic absolute. The result is poetry whose only subject is the psychology of the poet and whose final value is scientific; which is as it should be, since the snobbism responsible for it tries to treat poetry as if it were a science.

Poetry of this kind thus finally comes to justify itself by an analogy with mechanical reality. France and America provide numerous examples of it. In America industry itself may be said to have an imagination and so to furnish an instructive parallel to the creative mind faced with the problem of employing itself. If it cannot have poems which shall have a place in the world, perhaps it can have poems which shall have a place in themselves, which shall end where they begin; if it cannot have poetry, perhaps it can have purity. The machine is a practical symbol of automatism and may be said to create itself as the psychological poem does, to be its own product. Instead of possessing a life, such a poem possesses a mechanism, a fixed emotional routine that may be called absolute because its effect never varies. In France the analogical element is provided to poetry by the mechanical principle of other arts, by painting, principally by music. The aesthetic purity of the poem is made to consist in its behaving like a machine, in imitating its making and in maintaining an absence of meaning except as a *non-conscious* cause and instrument of a conscious effect. The history of this theory lies between Poe, in whom it was an amateur's attempt to defend the independence of the poem on the grounds of its mere pleasure-reality, and Paul Valéry and other musicopoeticians, who further develop the pleasure-reality theory by transferring the centre of the poem from its origin in the poet to its conclusion in the reader. Invention is converted into reaction, poetry into criticism. The pure poem is arrived at by subtracting the poem from itself. Only its limits remain, its points of origin and of communication. The rest is a time and space necessity between them, the place, presumably, which the poetic mind leaves to be filled in by the contemporary mind; the myth, once more, which the contemporary mind is supposed to suggest to the poetic mind, but now a blank myth, since the contemporary mind believes itself to have arrived at the all-in-all, that what is not itself is merely its shadow.

If, in spite of the present surquidry of the contemporary mind and the accidie with which the poetic mind is afflicted, it were possible to conceive of the production of a true poem, to what should we look for evidences of its reality? To those inner circumstances which make up the poetic mind and which the poem is the means of externalizing, as the poetic mind is the means of externalizing the poem, which hitherto existed only unto itself. In this mutuality lies the real clue to the double reality of the poem, its truth as a poem, its truthfulness as a demonstration of the poet's mind. For we have now come to the point where it is permissible to talk of the poetic mind as the poet's mind, and of the poet's mind as the only contemporary mind possible in the poem, its incidental reality. The poem itself is supreme, above persons; judging rather than judged; keeping criticism at a respectful distance; it is even able to make a reader of its author. It comes to be because an individual mind is clear enough to perceive it and then to become its instrument. Criticism can only have authority over the poem if the poet's mind was from the start not sufficiently clear, sufficiently free of criticism; if it obeyed an existing, that is, a past order of reality, rather than a present order of reality, that is, the order of the things which do not yet exist. How shall this true poem be recognized? By those tests of reality it imposes on the reader; perhaps, then, only by the strength of the hostility it arises and the extent of its unpopularity even with the minority cults, or by its modest contentment with itself and the obscurity to which it is consigned.

False poems, as distinguished from weak poems, are those written to respond to tests of reality imposed by the contemporary mind and are therefore able to satisfy them better than any true one. The creative history of the false poem is the age, the author sensible of the age and the set of outer circumstances involved in his delicate adjustment to the age at a particular moment, in a particular place. Nothing remains beyond this, no life, no element, as in the true poem, untranslatable except in the terms provided by the poem itself. In the true poem these terms form a measurement that hitherto did not exist, and the test of the poem's reality is: to what degree is it a new dimension of reality? Indeed, in the true poem poetry is the science of reality, so-called science, itself the myth—the corpus of knowledge to which poetry has for centuries been an inspired drudge, turning it into the sensible material of a religious mysticism, a gross and flabby self-worship. Poetry, in other words, has been the divine solvent converting knowledge into truth, until knowledge, mad with its own modernity, declared itself the sole source of truth. But if knowledge can dismiss poetry, can it dismiss the poet? If the poetic mind was once the source of truth for knowledge, does it cease to have truth because the corpus of knowledge finds it no longer useful? In its primitive period of usefulness to knowledge it was a superior *knowing*; itself truth, knowledge its truthfulness: the true poem was at once truth and myth (truthfulness), knowing and knowledge, reality and test of reality. But if knowledge is, so to speak, composing its own monster-poem, has the poem as such necessarily disappeared? Can minds and their perceptions be erased by a piece of self-investigated india-rubber?

The word *poem* itself is an ever new meaning of an ever new combination of *doing* and *making* as one act, with a third inference of *being* perpetuating these in dynamic form. The only difference between a poem and a person is that in a poem *being* is the final state, in a person the preliminary state. These two kinds of realities, that of the person, that of the poem, stand at one end and the other of the poet's mind, which is but progressive experience made into a recurrent sequence circulating between one kind of reality and the other without destroying one reality in the other.

T. S. Eliot observed some time ago that "the conditions which may be considered to be unfavourable to the writing of good poetry are unfavourable to the writing of good criticism."[20] This implies that the reality of poetry is externally, not internally derived. But though "conditions" may be unfavourably disposed to good poetry, they cannot affect the *writing* of good poetry if there are poets who insist on writing it. They can, however, affect the writing of such poetry as is actually created by external contemporary conditions; poetry, in fact, that is not poetry at all but the by-product of a period's spiritual indecision. But such poetry is not a manifestation of the poetic mind but of certain unhappy formations in the contemporary mind acting as individuals whose task it is to present the signs of the times rather than poetry.

We have, then, in a period when the Zeitgeist, the Old Man of the Sea, is working particular mischief, a number of Sinbads drifting at large whose fate it is to be at the mercy of his humours. They may either be washed astride a breakwater (when their balancing gestures are called criticism) or dashed over the sea wall into the Sacred Grove, where they try to feel at home in spite of the Old Man on their back (when their balancing gestures are called poetry).

When such contemporary formations are converted into creative or critical personalities by Zeitgeist humours, a subtle strangeness will, of course, be perceived in them. First something scarcely discernible, except for the feeling of embarrassment it conveys—a faint, but distinct foreign accent; next that dissociation or snobbism which a newly converted Catholic feels toward the born Catholic, or the cabinet-maker who has learned his trade at a school toward one who has inherited it from his father. It is the self-conscious earnestness of an alien doing his best to become acclimatized to his adopted country. Without that natural endowment which makes the creative faculty indifferent to moral justifications of itself (its moral justification being best presented in a work), the chief preoccupation of the factitious creative personality is with the moral values, or the legitimacy, of literature. A blend is thus made of the creative and critical operations, resulting in much interesting self-revelation ("good criticism"), but in too much dull self-concealment in poetry, which comes to be the martyrdom of lack-of-confidence-in-self. Mr. Eliot's axiom, therefore, which was composed long before he was completely floored by the Zeitgeist, must be brought up-to-date in this way: "The conditions which may be considered favourable to the writing of good criticism may be considered favourable to the writing of good criticism." For in such language poetry is but an incident of criticism. Mr. Eliot wrote several years ago: "Every form of genuine criticism is directed toward creation. The historical or the philosophical critic of poetry is criticising poetry in order to create a history or a philosophy; the poetic critic is criticising poetry in order to create poetry."[21] In a review of two books by two distinguished contemporary personalities, Mr. Herbert Read and M. Ramon Fernandez, in the October, 1926, issue of the *New Criterion* (a community of contemporary personalities), Mr. Eliot goes still further: "The significance of the term critic has varied indefinitely; in our time the most vigorous critical minds are philosophical minds, are, in short, creative of values."[22]

Further characteristics of this snobbism, besides its preoccupations with the moral values of literature, are its emphasis on personal pedigree, learning and literary internationalism. The review referred to above is so generous in examples of these that I cannot refrain from using it as a text, nor indeed this entire number of the *New Criterion*, which includes an essay by M. Fernandez himself beginning, "It is pleasant for a French critic to write for the cultivated public on the other side of the Channel"; a poem by Mr. Read himself, *The Lament of Saint Denis* with a motto *From the Institutes of Johann Lorenz von Mosheim, translated by Archibald Maclaine* (1764) and three foot-notes: *Inferno xxviii.* 121–2, *Paradiso: x.* 94, and *Boëthius: De Consolatione, II., vi.*, the learned if not the moral justifications for such lines as

And then a faint rumour in the night
An approaching murmur of enemies
Their hearts were suddenly loud in their still bodies
Fluttering wildly within those livid tunicles of flesh

(poor Mr. Read, likewise floored by the Zeitgeist, who in his less contemporaneous days could write less ambitiously but more authentically:

Judas was right
In a mental sort of way;
For he betrayed another and so
With purpose was self-justified.
But I delivered my body to fear—
I was a bloodier fool than he.);[23]

and a poem by Mr. Eliot himself, *Fragment of a Prologue*, with two mottoes, one from the *Choephoroi*, the other from St. John of the Cross, the poem itself being a kind of epilogue to *Ulysses*, or Ulysses in the Waste Land.

But the review itself is even more illuminating, especially as to the love of pedigree, learning and literary internationalism: "Mr. Read and M. Fernandez provide an excellent example of this invalidation of the ancient classification" (critical and creative) because, the next sentence continues, "They are of the same generation, of the same order of culture; their education is as nearly the same as that of men of different race and nationality can be. . . . Both were primarily students of literature, and animated by the desire to find a meaning and justification for literature. Mr. Read has the advantage of being European and English; M. Fernandez that of being European and American (he was born in Mexico). . . . Both are critics with international learning and international standards." All this to prove the invalidation of that "ancient" classification.

It is improper to advance that criticism and poetry spring from the same kind of personal impulse, unless it is made equally clear that they must diverge at an early stage toward their respective positions. Criticism and creation do not face the same way, but face each other, criticism forgoing creation in order to be able to describe it. This purpose demands learning in criticism, because it is thus the author not of one poem, let us say, but of the history of one poem and another and another (since when face to face with one poem the critic sees many others as well); but it does not mean that criticism may be substituted for creation, as would follow if that "ancient classification" were really invalidated. The novel perhaps shows the danger of such a substitution more clearly than any other kind of writing, being avowedly critical rather than creative, historical rather than poetic: it is a description of poetic reality by contemporary reality. Wherever the novel tries to create poetic values, it becomes false art, as with Proust, Joyce, Virginia Woolf and such American poetic novelists as Waldo Frank and Sherwood Anderson. For, while the novel may suggest them or describe them, it needs to be emphasized dogmatically that there are no true creative values but poetic values—values which can be final without reference to their contemporary setting. (This does not apply to the *poetical* novel, to Borrow or Melville, *poetical* referring only to the character of the style, not to the creative intention of the novel.) The novel may be eminently true, or truthful, but it is not truth; and no novelist who held his work in proper respect would claim it to be truth except in this relative sense of truthful. If Mr. Eliot were not so comfortably relaxing against the novel, "a capital point for every contemporary mind (*sic*)"[24] (to start from), evidently because it can be perverted to bring about "this invalidation of the ancient classification," he would perhaps reject Proust with Mr. Read and M. Fernandez not so much because Proust was wanting in the moral element as because he falsified the novel—composing it synthetically of those infinitesimal morsels of poetic reality by which the connoisseur's palate has had to appear uniformly stimulated throughout that long, long from-egg-to-apple dinner.

Proust recalls the snobbism of literary inter-nationalism, which has provided Charles Scott-Moncrieff, George Moore and Ezra Pound among others, with continuous employment. Any serious indictment of it would only assist in prolonging the sufferings of the silent populations whose palates were long ago exhausted by foreign banqueting but who go on because the connoisseurs go on, who go on because they are at the head of the table and cannot escape. Excepting rare instances of personal sympathy with a foreign language arising out of associations, of circumstance or temperament; excepting also such a unique case of internationalism as that of America and England, where one is but a historical layer of the other; any persistent cultivation of a contemporary foreign literature is a snobbism inspired, apart from its association with a general programme of literary snobbism, by a romantic purpose to find relief from one dull literary scene in another—a form of literary pornography. Nothing could be more alien to Mr. Eliot's temperament, for example, than the sentiment and temperament expressed in: "la littérature est impossible. Il faut en sorter" which he quotes from Jean Cocteau's letter to Jacques Maritain on poetry and religion. "International standards" of literature are a degraded critical Esperanto and, like Esperanto, comprehensible only to Esperantists.

What unites *littérateurs* (the successors of the critics and creators of "the ancient classification") in this generation is, in fact, not standards of taste or positive intellectual sympathy, but the feeling of panic occasioned by the setting adrift of literature by the time-universe. The reason why contemporary critics are so interested in inquiring into the nature of the function of literature is not, as Mr. Eliot suggests, because they do not wish "to take for granted a whole universe," but because a whole universe has given literature its dismissal papers.[25] Naturally endowed creative writers may protect themselves from the present Zeitgeist or remain entirely unaffected by it. But those sensitive spots in the contemporary mind to be identified as *littérateurs* can neither avoid nor revoke the Zeitgeist nor yet cancel themselves, since they are so organically of the Zeitgeist; and are thus obliged to make a religion of their own posthumousness, a religion so serious that Mr. Eliot himself calls it "an athleticism, a *training*, of the soul as severe and ascetic as the training of the body of a runner."[26] The asceticism on which it is based is the deprivation of the universe which science has forced on literature; and the moral values implied are the coward's promise to keep up his courage though all is lost.

The most redeeming and yet most unfortunate characteristic of this snob-criticism is its seriousness. Unfortunate because by contrast with the complete frivolousness or inaneness of all other contemporary critical writing it is the only criticism that demands any respect from the independent writer; and in this way likely to make him, in spite of his independence, ingenuously shy of it, and of expressing his normal reactions to the awful gloom that it has cast over the whole literary scene. Such is the science of overwhelming by pomp. Even the *London Mercury* would not if it could quiz the *New Criterion*, but would on the contrary feel flattered to be counted amongst its colleagues.

The final effect of this snobbism is the deliberate cultivation of a modernity, a calculated and therefore more "classical" quality ("We live") than mere crude romantic contemporaneousness ("I'm glad I'm alive" or "I'm sorry I'm alive"). "A poem which was never modern will not pass into that curious state of suspended animation by means of which the poems we call classic are preserved active to the palate," said Edgell Rickword, Editor of the *Calendar of Modern Letters*, lately next to the *New Criterion* the most serious community of contemporary personalities.[27] Thus poetic modernism, advertised by its own uplift, reaches the poetry societies of the provinces, who by now have used up all their war and post-war subjects and are grateful for a change. "At an evening of the Bournemouth Poetry Society," reports the

Bournemouth Echo, "held at Eight Bells, Christchurch, poetry enthusiasts (one came all the way from Broadstone) were well rewarded by a remarkably live and able paper by Mrs. Leslie Goodwin on 'Further Aspects of Modern Poetry.' Mrs. Goodwin called attention to the unappreciated importance of the Left Wing or extreme Modernist Group, who have new ideas as to what is appropriate and beautiful." For the Old Man of the Sea must have his joke.

"Modern," however, is not a contemporary invention: it must not be forgotten that the *littérateurs* of the characteristic eighteenth century were likewise modernists and likewise invalidated "the ancient classification." Their poetry and criticism, although not born of the same impulse, were written from the same point of view, which gave them a mutual consistency if not a reciprocal power. Criticism became, then also, a moral measurement: arbitrary judgments for arbitrary poetic practices. Poetry was a critical convenience, criticism a poetic convenience; the offspring of this union between them had that inbred half-reality which is characteristic of present-day manifestations of the contemporary mind in criticism and poetry. The period was a "literary" period. It had been fitting, for example, for Milton some time before, to dedicate *Samson Agonistes* to a campaign against what he called the corrupt gratification of the people with "comic stuff," and to a classical conception and treatment of tragedy. It was fitting for Whitman, long after, to justify *Leaves of Grass* by an exactly contrary critical attitude: "that the real test applicable to a book is entirely outside literary tests."[28] For, though both disregarded the meaning of poetic intention, one accepted the authority of literature, the other that of life and humanity. The authority of eighteenth-century literature was neither of these, but a working compromise between them. Literature was the rationalizing apparatus that added logic to morality; life, the literary demonstration. This code expressed the temper of the age faithfully: snobbism, or conformity of behaviour to a degree where nothing happened at all, where important poetry was prevented from happening. Such literary sterility caused a reaction in the next century, frenzied fertility resulting in an unpedigreed stock. Although a fresh creative basis was found, the preceding century furnished its literary ancestry, which could be revolted against but not cast out of the blood. So poetry was for a time a romantic misfit, until new critical values could be found to match the new poetical values. In Keats we find many Pope-ish echoes; as we find many nineteenth-century echoes in the poetry of Miss Sitwell. Torn between her inherited Wordsworthianisms and Tennysonianisms and her acquired Pope-isms, her poetry no less than Keats' bears the marks of a conflict. Her nineteenth- century-isms (as Keats' eighteenth-century-isms) it is possible to indulge because they were inherited; likewise her Gallicisms, as a decorative relief to these. But why should Miss Sitwell, with an abundantly endowed creative faculty, find it necessary to praise *The Rape of the Lock* as a beautiful example "of the fusion of subject matter and style"?[29] If not because prevailing critical snobbisms force the independent creative faculty to strengthen its pedigree with artificial critical values which, in turn, act as a kind of protective snobbism (as Elizabethanisms did for Keats).

Nineteenth-century poetry, after a brief period of sentimental debate, failed to develop any real critical values. Instead, it borrowed its titles from the idea of progress, the philosophical demiurge of the century, thus only changing one social god for another without the disguise this time of a literary mask. The popular mode of mysticism resulting from this religiosity was the intelligence—not the intellect. The reason why the intellect is held anti-religious is that it is an individual property rather than a social one and is therefore less likely to accept as final the generalizations of the prevailing community system of faith. Contemporary criticism is endeavouring to elevate the mass-intelligence by making it behave like an independent intellect, the effect of which is to rob the term *intellectual integrity* of all significance. While "contemporary" eighteenth-century poetry cannot be said to have had great intellectual integrity, it did make an honest compromise between the general intelligence and the individual intellect by postulating *wit* as the common raw material of literature. However wit may be abused by being made to serve moral ends, it is in itself an intellectual competence which is bound to protect itself in some way against the uses to which it is put. *Wit* may indeed be called the subject-matter of the best of eighteenth-century poetry, as human wisdom forms the subject-matter of the worst of nineteenth-century poetry.

In the earlier period there was at least wit to act as a basis, however artificial, of critical values. In the later there was only a standard of philosophical satisfaction demanding an unrestrained flattering of every possible variety of human activity: poetry being the spiritual sign of practical prosperity and advance, the personified muse of optimism. For this later tendency Wordsworth's critical commonplaces were principally responsible; which even modern writers find it impossible to reject on the proper ground. Miss Sitwell, for example, thinks that it is time to discard the Wordsworthian tradition, not because it is fundamentally false, but only because it has grown dull in the course of its development. It is time to leave "the peasant and words suitable to the peasant." That is, what poetry needs is a general correction of taste, not an independence in which creative values have a lack of conformity according to the variety of poetic minds (the use of *poetic mind* as a critical abstraction is likely to make us forget that it is *a* rather than *the* poetic mind). It is a telling piece of well-meaning literary snobbism to call

Wordsworth a peasant poet. Wordsworth, like Miss Sitwell, wanted to "interest mankind" in the proper way, "to correct the present state of the public taste in this country." "Humble and rustic life was generally chosen" because it made a more fluid philosophical language for poetry: the peasant flavour is only a literary manner, as that part of Miss Sitwell's own poetry which is dedicated to taste is but the exploitation of a literary manner. Wordsworth's poetry is no more fit for reading by peasants than Miss Sitwell's is by princesses. Both have the view that poetry is a careful annotation of life. To Wordsworth, poetry is "the spontaneous overflow of powerful feelings"; to Miss Sitwell, it brings "new and heightened consciousness to life."[30] Both have a purpose to deal with what she calls the "common movement of life," only "the modern poet has a different stylisation." Wordsworth, under the false mask of taste, made moral enlargements on trivial subjects. The modern poet who, like Miss Sitwell, is not overwhelmed by the world or made an instrument of the Zeitgeist, but who in spite of his contempt for its blustering demonstration of power clings to it out of an inherited and old-fashioned sense of duty, wastes himself on that sentimental, self-sacrificing office which Miss Sitwell calls "showing the world in all its triviality."

So that present modernism is not even literary in the eighteenth-century sense but a complex of pietist snobberies and sentimentalities.

V: Poetry and Progress

In spite of "the invalidation of that ancient classification" (between the critic and the creator), to quote T. S. Eliot once more, contemporary criticism shows certain survivals of the humble advisory or research functions of criticism in the past: it continues to make a few naive medical recommendations. On the one hand, we find the new universe of science, the successor of the old politico-philosophistical universe, forcing literature to retire or to show good cause why it should not or to temporize in elaborate leave-takings. On the other, we find science hopefully recommended as a new poetical subject. Even so presumably modern a type as the intelluptuous Aldous Huxley still clings to the superstition of subject-matter and, while regretting "the deplorable traditionalism of subject-matter that weighs so heavily upon so much of contemporary poetry," reaffirms Wordsworthianism by suggesting new subject-matter. Overlooking the fact that subject- matter has always exhausted rather than nourished creative energy, he names science as the proper modern subject for poetry and Laforgue as a poet who made real poetry out of science, "science's only lyrist."[31] Now Laforgue is, as a matter of fact, one of the most non-subject of poets. He did, indeed, attempt to make poetry a discursive record of pure sensation—*comme parlé*. His *Complaintes* are a series of satires on subjects, an anthology of phraseologies; and science can only mean to poetry one more phraseology. His intention was to give poetry complete ideological freedom from subjects, to record sensation in its natural sense-terms, in its immediate, or contemporary, associations, without resorting to literary classification. Such poetry makes use of science to help it invent special vocabularies, but it does not use science as a subject. It would indeed be, in the scientist's opinion, romantically unscientific. It is not "scientific" to speak of the sun as white as tap-room spittle, or to speak of the moon as having its ears stopped with cotton. It is merely the effort of an intellectually non-intellectual intellect to describe contemporary emotions with contemporary sophistication but with a classical affectation of innocence. Such is the Anti-Reason of Paul Valéry and such is that vocabularistic whimsicality or quaintness by which poets like E. E. Cummings and Edith Sitwell inoculate themselves against the Zeitgeist—a protective measure against the practical mentalism of their period with which poets are always afraid of becoming emotionally infected.

Expressionism—and all super-realist movements may be classified as expressionistic—is another typical recommendation, a starvation diet as a protest against the tyranny of the material universe, a denial of the potency of inorganic matter. Technically, expressionism admits no distinction between the word and the poetic mind. The word, not the mind, becomes the centre of poetic life. It acts without memory, without equipment; it is completely unqualified, capable of expressing anything it chooses at the moment to express. This autonomous quality of words may justify itself in the academic nursery prose of Gertrude Stein, but it is futile in poetry because, though words must be pure in poetry, they cannot be blank. Expressionism therefore may have been valuable as a temporary rest-and-diet cure, but in general it resulted in creative depression. For as it is difficult for an invalid to resist technical preoccupation with himself, so expressionism encouraged morbid egotism and imbecile healthiness. Instead of transferring the creative centre from the poetic mind to words, it should have concentrated on the rehabilitation of the poetic mind, with words as the physical incident of this mind. Words in themselves are as false a distinction as is the body in itself apart from the mind.

Expressionism was merely one complete illustration of this unholy alliance in which the Zeitgeist kills and criticism cures. It passed, and the Zeitgeist is still killing, criticism still curing. The expressionist objected to the destruction of the personal self in a world becoming more and more material and externalized. So he shut out the visible world and invented an abstract self to replace that self which is only a product of the external world—the Zeitgeist-self. Expressionism, or some similar movement of "objective" subjectivity, is therefore likely to flourish when the Zeitgeist is patently destructive rather than constructive, as in war- and post-war Germany. But the expressionist is one thing, expressionism is another. The expressionist is a personal victim, expressionism a critical device of the Zeitgeist for allowing its victim to extinguish itself.

The pragmatic reality of the Zeitgeist and its criticism must be assumed, as must that of anything by which the weakness of one set of minds prevails over the weakness of another. All that can be said for critics who serve the Zeitgeist is that some, the most stupid, know not what they do. The critics who know what they do never stoop to critical recommendation but consecrate their intelligence to the complete service of the Zeitgeist. Poetry must not be assisted, it must conform. If it cannot conform it must cease to exist, since it can only exist by a kindly dispensation from the Zeitgeist. Zeitgeist intelligence, as it is possessed by criticism, thus returns poetry to its primitive ritualistic function of community revelation. In other words, it is the generalized voice of social sentiment: as an independent personal attribute it is, in fact, non-existent. It ceases to employ subject-matter not because it has renounced its job as an inspired research-worker on matter that philosophy, history and science could take no further, but because it has been denied subjectivity and once and for all universalized; given, instead of subject-matter in various stages of indigestion, the whole self-digested substance of contemporary learning and asked to humble itself before it in reverent self-revilement. First of all, of course, searching itself to see if it is sufficiently pure, that is, if it has really acknowledged itself a worm in its god's sight: in which purification criticism condescends to assist by what is called discovering to literature its function.

Science, then, as a critical recommendation for poetry is as irrelevant as an attack on science for impeding the progress of poetry. For science as agent of a period's mass-vanity is one thing and science as a small historical item is another; and most contemporary views of science overlook the second sense in favour of the first. Only the first is, indeed, apparent, since science cannot afford to allow the second to appear: never has it been more reckless, more blind, more disorganized, more meaningless than at the present moment, never, therefore, more in need of being accepted as truth instead of as a small though authoritative corner of human knowledge. The best way to hide confusion and flippancy is to declare a new life or age, to proclaim a Zeitgeist. Poetry as creative truth is thus made to apologize for itself because, being a personal attribute, it seems irregular and behind the times. The advance of time as a universal force superior to persons left the time of the individual far behind long ago. Intelligence, the historical fallacy, is the philosophical means by which the individual makes his literal time catch up with the figurative synthetic time of the totality of matter. Advanced contemporary poetry is thus breathless with scholarship—the *Waste Land*, a poem of four hundred and thirty-three lines, has one learned reference to every eight of these; but it is not breathless with intellect—there is no sign of intellect *per se* in the *Waste Land*. For as soon as an independent mental act needs to substantiate itself historically it ceases to be independent and it ceases to be intellect. It is only rather evasively intelligent.

Such is the time-fear and such is the timidity of personal illusion against gross illusion, or of common sense as individual wisdom against the doctrinaire Common Sense of the knowledge-superstition. So does the quantity of learning separate itself from its source and so does the independence of the mind become the source of its own subjection. What is being fed to poetry now is the dregs of what poetry itself has produced, and produced long ago. Or, let us not say poetry, since it is a word spoiled by self-abuse. More specifically: science or any similar fetish of the concrete intelligence is a mere by-the-way of the suggestive intelligence, or intellect, a digression that becomes more and more irrelevant and wanting in meaning as it treats itself as a whole instead of as an enlarged incident of the suggestive intelligence. The nearer it seems to approach a whole, the more vain, the more blind it will become, the nearer it is approaching collapse. Modern warfare is only a small aspect of the decay of science, "scientific" spiritualism another. Sooner or later, sooner than expected, science will confound itself with its own successes and remain only an old-fashioned household word. Its present prestige is due chiefly to its imperfection: when every cure has been found for everything and every device for doing everything has been invented and all the Florence Nightingale-sentiment showered on scientists has been used up, it will be clear how much sidetracked poetry went into the making of science. And poetry, as the suggestive intelligence, will probably then make some new suggestion for human energy at a loss as to how to employ itself; and will be once more put in its place until this digression, in turn, wears itself out.

Meanwhile, however, science and its accessories are the new life and poetry is the old, which must either acknowledge itself as dead or consent to have itself kept alive by gland extracts, Viennese rejuvenation treatments and radium, as a testimony of the power and grace of science. There have been isolated and faint protests from poets against Zeitgeist superstition, but in the main poets and especially critics have grasped the possibilities of contemporary success in Zeitgeist vanity and dedicated poetry to a display of its own helplessness and to a vulgar flattery of the contemporary god, learned matter. But how low in spirits and how full of humility! The only joy-in-life left to contemporary Zeitgeist poetry is a little half-hearted obscenity; and even obscenity must apologize for itself with learning.

To propose that contemporary learning retards the synthesis always implicit in poetry, to point out that it is science which is slow, and not poetry, would confess a view of the nature of poetry incompatible with the self—deprecating sophistication of present Zeitgeist poetry and criticism; and immediately ally one with that sentimental adoration of poetry common to clergymen, poetry societies, editors of weekly literary reviews, anthologists, anthology readers, university professors, business men, doctors and modern lyrical poets. To say, with Francis Thompson, that poetry is always a hundred years in advance of science would seem equally trivial, because Francis Thompson is not a respectable literary reference, although his extravagance in paying homage to an ancient dogmatic institution was more dignified than the extravagance of contemporary poetry and criticism in paying homage to an ephemeral, dogmatic Zeitgeist.[32] In truth, advance is an unfortunate word: poetry does not advance except in the sense that other things, such as science, are behind it. There is no progress of poetry any more than there is a progress of time. There is a progress of matter, but this is a permanent progress of corruption.

Indeed, any attempt to look to a personal rather than to an academic dignity in poetry will be set down to critical romanticism. Why any-thing is less true than otherwise if it can be set down to critical romanticism must remain a mystery. For snob-critics make a practice of annulling the value of any statement detrimental to them by giving it a name which relieves them of the obligation of replying to it directly.

(The late T. E. Hulme tried to rescue the artist from historical difficulties by combining art and philosophy into a dry theory of historical objectivity. Instead of delivering him up to time he brought time inside the bounds of the creative system that he outlined. He advocated a discipline that would control both time and the creator through the impersonal severity, the absoluteness, in which artistic forms might be conceived. The product of this "objective" objectivity is therefore pure, hard, non-sympathetic. It is not intelligent: that is, it is not materialistically interpretative, but material. It is not emotional: that is, it is not imaginatively imitative but unimaginatively representational. It is a non-human object. But such a system results only in criticism, not in works. It expresses an attitude toward time, protests against extraneous elements which have crept into art, states the conflict between art and civilization, between creative isolation and vulgarized originality. It shows the creator defeated by progress taking refuge in a petulant barbarism.)[33]

Social sentiment is the general source, conscious or unconscious, of the "subjects" of poetry. Contemporary social interests may even, as at present, deprive poetry of an old stock of subjects and, instead of providing a new stock, require that the inspiration of poetry shall be even its own poverty, its humble renouncement of worldliness after it has been frustrated by worldliness. What causes a change, then, in the official inspiration of poetry is usually not a revolt on the part of poetry itself against the tyranny of social sentiment, but the absorption of poetry by a new social sentiment, which uses it as an aggressive weapon against the old. The extravagant modernism of poetry at any particular moment is due not to its independent defiance of superannuated social sentiment but to its excessive slavishness and adaptability, by which it anticipates, and thus seems to invent, an impending social sentiment about to make itself historically effective. Literature, poetry in particular, is in this way an instrument for dramatizing the historical conflict between an old social sentiment and a new. It performs the work of transition which might otherwise be accomplished with greater violence. Spiritual violence in poetry makes the least tangible sort of wreckage, because the formal cathartic process is considered natural to it and disintegrating forces in it easily simulate catharsis; also because the superstition of form imposes on it an artificial urbanity. It is difficult, besides, for the vanity which so often goes with poetic powers to resist the occasions for theatricality which the Zeitgeist drama provides.

So it is fitting that Mr. Edwin Muir should call a book dealing with the work of characteristic writers of to-day *Transition*,[34] a descriptive term having to do with social sentiment rather than with literary criticism; and that he should fail with those writers to whom the Zeitgeist is not a literary clue, just where, in fact, literary criticism is demanded. But the distinction between literary criticism and social sentiment (Zeitgeist sentiment), between unconditioned poetry and conditioned poetry, becomes vague when the snobbism of progress, disguised as literary modernism, obscures the anarchic nature of creative activity and tries to justify it to its time by showing that it is an effect of history. In this normalizing and levelling of literature to its age, any poet who does not seem to conform to the historical laws of his age is rejected by social sentiment disguised as literary criticism. Poetry is required to proceed not from an individual sense of life but from a social sense of literature: it must emphasize the social rather than the individual origin of creation. It must, that is, be a vehicle of prophecy of the most brutally servile kind.

The revolt against nineteenth-century subjects was the sign that a new social sentiment was preparing to displace the old, using literature as a destroying agency, as it had been used as a constructive agency in the beginnings of the Victorian period. (The sensitiveness of the creative mind is thus seen as an accursed talent, since by it the poet may become so open to influences that he ceases to create and is, instead, merely a historical barometer; in periods of change the public-utility character of creation is likely to overshadow completely its private character.) The Victorian period consolidated a great many different sets of values already loosely equated—economic values, religious values, moral values, aesthetic values, and so forth. Social values were the general mean of all these. Then material development began to demand a more flexible social sentiment, a more "broad-minded" interpretation and differentiation of values. Literature made the first efforts at formal differentiation by attempting to separate moral values from aesthetic values.

The effect of playing this historical role was to make literature digress first into pure sociology, continuing in this century in such anachronisms as Butler, Shaw, Wells, Galsworthy and finally D. H. Lawrence (an instance of contemporary Rousseauism); then into an anti-social orgy of third-rate decadence—both of these resulting from the differentiation of moral and aesthetic values. The virtue, however, of both literary sociology and literary decadence is that sooner or later they must write themselves out. The former lasted longer because it is more congenial to the Anglo-Saxon temperament, the latter died out soon after it was contracted from French decadence. In the English 'nineties there was no decadence anywhere except in literature. In France, on the other hand, there is always decadence, it is the great national genius and source of life. The French have, indeed, a natural aptitude for decadence; it is in them a sign of health. The underlying theme of all French literature, romantic and classical alike, is Decline, and all French writers of excellence must begin by falling in love with Decline. This is why French criticism has no difficulty in reconciling contradictory literary movements, since they are all in agreement on at least one point.

So it is pitiful to think of Arthur Symons, a feeble English decadent, making brotherly advances to such healthy French decadents as Baudelaire and Laforgue. The sociologists, though here and there slightly infected with decadence, were for the most part healthy, cheerful and good. William Morris and Edward Carpenter were the early poetical writers of the sociological movement, whose literature soon, however, lost its poetical tinge and became propagandist, journalistic, scientific, philosophical or witty. Doughty was perhaps the writer who paid least attention to contemporary social sentiment. Even Hardy was contaminated, on one side by historical mysticism, rural economy and the divorce laws, on the other by the same decadent, sentimental suicidism which made Barrie, because he was Scotch, simply a pretty writer. The decadents were divided into two classes, the sad people, the bad people. Among the sad people were Thomson, Dowson, Davidson, Middleton and O'Shaughnessy, who may all be described in the adjective invented by Max Beerbohm for Enoch Soames: *dim*. The bad people were the unmentionables who collapsed, too weak for vice, at the feet of the Zeitgeist.

Though literary sociology survived literary decadence, it soon merged with non-literary forces; and though literature continued as one of the minor branches of social intelligence, poetry as idiosyncratic creation officially disappeared. What literature did persist was unimportant, as there was now no historical reason for its being otherwise. In the Victorian period literature had been an instrument of hypocrisy. When a more liberal rationalism succeeded Victorian rationalism, literature became merely an instrument for confessing hypocrisy, especially poetic hypocrisy. One doubtful result of this was that the quality of poetry went into other kinds of writing and effected a great revival of wit in the sophisticated novel and essay. Sentimental reactions to the passing of poetry then occurred, without the attendance of criticism, in great variety—Georgianism, Imagism, Vers Librism, lyricism, all too wanting in originality or direction to survive their own enthusiasm. At last criticism was awakened by the voice of the new Zeitgeist, which was one in which the only social excuse that could be found for poetry was in its renunciation of its non-tribal, personal attributes. But as the new universe in which this perfunctory occupation had been found for poetry had no real need even for a formal act of renunciation by it, criticism, in evoking a new social sentiment, was asking for a hypocrisy in poetry more inexcusable than Victorian hypocrisy, which was at least the result of a real social need. Worse still, not only was poetry called upon to exchange private poetic reality for public contemporary reality, but even the contemporary reality of the time-universe was received second-hand. For the time-universe having haughtily dismissed poetry, criticism was obliged to invent an analogical universe, a sort of scholastic image before which poetry could perform its prostrations.

As in any time there exist a number of unclassified minds capable of much but wanting in personal differentiation, such an equivocal definition of poetry opens up for them an unlimited opportunity for converting want of person into ritualistic impersonality. In this manner does the disintegration of poetry as a thing of poets make poets of minds that had otherwise been nameless thought-mechanisms. The mechanistic side of contemporary Zeitgeist poetry is shown in its complete lack of form in any organic sense—though it maintains an automatic convention of formality. It is obliged to forswear all personal reality (unless it can be classified as "psychological"), to submerge itself in contemporary realism, to employ a learned ritual in which contemporary data are left unpoetized, that is, as in their final stage of truth. This definition of poetry is further observed by reviving previous literary rites, though rejecting the various historical realisms with which they were connected for the present realism: uniting the historical past and the historical present in one expanded social sentiment, an authoritative snobbism against creative personal eccentricity. The official seriousness and dignity of this sentiment acting as literary criticism is likely to obscure the fact that it is but the old snobbism of non-poets (literary poets) against poets (non-literary poets).

VI: The Higher Snobbism

The true relations between society and poetry are concealed by a number of reciprocal snobbisms which maintain an armed peace between them. It is the strength of snobbisms to be never at war with one another. The original snobbism in these relations obviously came from society. The poet was a man apart, foolish but tribally useful, and regarded with that half-fear and half-contempt which the executive or active members of a community tend always to have for the divining or reflective members. If we imagine the poet in an extremely unsuspicious attitude toward his official rôle, we can see him as being probably without a retaliative or protective snobbism. But as society comes to depend less and less on the poet, as he is supplanted by patriotism, formal learning and other instruments of community self-reliance, his official dignity turns into a mere decorative social survival. Society loses fear of him, retaining only tender contempt. And the poet himself therefore emphasizes more and more the eccentric personal character of poetry and sets up a counter-snobbism, a pride in weakness and eccentricity, which plays on certain ancient superstitions about poetry that still survive. The formal corpus of these superstitions by which poetry remains a minor religion to society is criticism. Society represents practicality, against which poetry protects itself by cultivating an atmosphere of unpracticality. For society spares what is unpractical if it is made poetical. And the poet keeps up his illusion of self-respect under a cloak of salvaged history and legend, a Joseph's coat, a patchwork quilt of fact and fancy that grows a little shabbier from generation to generation, from age to age. Keats so fancied himself in the priestly Joseph's coat that he sacrificed himself to ambition, writing according to a layman's idea of how a poet should write, catering to society's snobbism toward poetry and to poetry's protective snobbism toward society. Many another independent genius has been led astray by the same flamboyant appeal.

Here within the ranks of poetry itself a reaction occurs against its increasing effeminacy and, without discarding their ancient prerogatives, poets enter into friendly competition with society in the manly arts. But this remains a subordinate snobbism, the signs of growth of shame and of decay. The whole snobbism by which poetry first came to terms with society is a gross snobbism still obtaining where poetry and society have not yet caught up with the Zeitgeist, or sometimes even continuing, from literary habit, where they have. Although the knowledge-display in advanced contemporary poetry has other more important explanations, it is to a small degree a survival of the superstitious practice of allusion, the *Golden Bough* supplanting the *Historical Library* of Diodorus Siculus, the Bestiaries, Ovid and so forth.

The next step is the breaking away, from the professionalism of the gross snobbism, of individual poets or groups of poets; whose counter-snobbism to the gross snobbism is their amateurishness, and to society a snobbism against its acquiescence in the gross snobbism. These amateurs protect themselves by exquisiteness: Pre-Raphaelite exquisiteness is a genuine example of non-professionalism in the Victorian period, Pater-Ruskin exquisiteness (to be counted as poetry because it was "poetical") a spurious one, being Victorianism in exotic trappings. In the end the gross snobbism generally reabsorbs the amateur snobbism by means of criticism.

Soon, however, society reaches a stage of such self-importance that it feels it beneath its dignity to carry on any longer its tender play with poetry. It abandons its snobbism of tolerance towards poetry and, except that small portion of contemporary society which remains slightly in arrear of the date, drops it out altogether. Poetry in the old sense nevertheless continues to live, principally on memories, still wielding its anachronistic gross snobbism against an imaginary snobbism of society, still relying on criticism to make it socially effective.

In theory, poetry has officially passed. A new universe without poetry might be expected. But instead a new criticism arises to proclaim poetry because there is no poetry, a criticism which shares the new universe's atavistic hunger for poetry. A poetry results that has a paradoxical reality, the contemporary reality which denies poetry's rights to existence, as having only a private personal reality or an official unreality—both equally unreal when viewed historically. This new poetry, born of the new criticism, attempts to placate the Zeitgeist by abandoning all the superstitions by which the old poetry prolonged its life, and by using against itself all the snobbisms that have ever been held toward poetry, including the last conclusive one, that there is no more poetry—all forming the higher snobbism, poetry's snobbishness toward itself. For creation it substitutes a philosophical life in the

Zeitgeist; for inspiration, criticism—the anti-poetic metaphysics of this life. Criticism and creation thus at last become single in act and in effect, immediately responding to social sentiment without intervening reflections or ecstasies. We are returned once more to the fitness of Mr. Eliot's observation on "the invalidation of that ancient classification" (between critic and creator).[35]

But although poetry in the old sense has theoretically passed, the personal idiosyncrasy that makes the poet cannot pass. Poetry quantitatively viewed is a social product; and one kind of social product may be superseded by another. But poetic power can only come from individuals and can only be superseded by itself in individuals. There are poets and there are authors of a social product, who are not poets. Contemporary thought tends to make all contemporary poetry a mere social product, handing over the task of invention to the higher snobbism. It unclasses the poet proper because his work might or might not form part of the social product. The ideal author of the social product is a correct citizen of his age. If the poet proper happens to have contemporary taste as well as poetic power he innocently becomes a spokesman for the higher snobbism.

Miss Sitwell, for example, unconsciously explains what the higher snobbism is really pining for: the respectable freedom of eighteenth-century literary Whiggery, where poetry could refine social sentiment without being forced to be poetry, where it could be professional without allying itself to the gross snobbism of romantic professionalism and where a minor criticism, at one with a minor poetry, could act as a social check against the poetry of a vulgar major criticism, against the gross snobbism. The higher snobbism is, in fact, in agreement with the new anti-poetic universe only in that it wishes to disconnect itself from the gross snobbism: even to disown poetry and substitute *letters*, in which poetry and criticism may be united if the contemporary intelligence is accepted as the philosophical life inspiring both. The higher snobbism is even willing to recommence a corrected poetic tradition, with the poet deprived of all those powers and privileges which in the beginning laid the foundations of the gross snobbism. If the poet is, it says, deprived of all the social importance granted him for being a poet, he will lose vulgarity; he will be part of a process, not a process in himself. He will not be a blustering, despised genius but a haughty, respected mechanic of contemporary thought.

Poetic power may even, as in Miss Sitwell's case, substitute taste for itself in order to be protected from the higher snobbism; it transfers itself from the tradition of personalities to the tradition of periods. This unnatural emphasis on periods rather than on poets has the effect of exaggerating the significance of poets who count for next to nothing in the tradition of personalities. What real sympathy can exist between the kangaroo Sitwell and the duck Beddoes? Yet Miss Sitwell is drawn to him: he is as close as she can come in the nineteenth century to her chosen literary past. He was one of the few eighteenth-century men of the first half of the nineteenth century; that is, he got as close to the eighteenth century as an early nineteenth-century character could. The closest he could get to the eighteenth century was the late Elizabethan drama, which he wrote like an eighteenth-century writer. Like Miss Sitwell he saw the problem of poetry as a problem of taste rather than of personality, the continuance of poetry as the continuance of the right tradition. He therefore picked up the Elizabethan drama where the eighteenth century left off with it—the eighteenth century never went much further in it than Shakespeare's lesser comedies and histories. Miss Sitwell finds herself an associate of Beddoes in literary heraldry; he is a fellow modernist carrying on with her, to quote Miss Sitwell, "the great tradition leading from the Elizabethans" in such lines as

> Old Adam, the carrion crow,
>   The old crow of Cairo;

slightly misquoted (or modernized?) by Miss Sitwell as

> Adam, that old carrion-crow
> Of Cairo.[36]

By thus naming herself with gentlemen rather than geniuses she puts herself beyond the suspicion of the higher snobbism; she makes herself a subject of the minor criticism, the criticism of breeding, rather than of the major criticism, the criticism of personality. Personality, Miss Sitwell would agree, is the glory of the commoner, and every charwoman a subject of the major criticism. In the contemporary situation the poet has to be either a Beddoes or an elevated charwoman: he boasts either a sense of literature (of time) or a sense of life—if the latter, he is an ostracized vulgarian of character.

The weakest point in the higher snobbism (and its criticism) is that in attacking the gross snobbism (and its criticism) it loses all sense of differentiation. Not only must a poet choose categorically between being a higher snob or a gross snob, because the minor criticism makes only these two large critical generations; but in its desire to destroy the gross snobs of contemporary literature it condescends to excuse certain poets of the past of gross snobbism, also certain contemporary poets who profess the gross snobbism, but as in the past—to excuse anyone, that is, who may be used against contemporary gross snobbism.

The minor criticism can therefore tolerate Dr. Bridges and Mr. Kipling better than it can some one who is a gross snob and a modern as well or some one who is a modern and, though not a gross snob, still not a higher one. It is only a matter of time until the higher snobbism adopts Tennyson, to take him away, as everything it can lay its hands on, from the gross snobbism. Thus Miss Sitwell, in attacking Mr. Alfred Noyes, Mr. J. G. Squire and Mr. Edward Shanks and the whole Yellow Press of poetry, falls back into the arms of Wordsworth. For she has, for the moment, in her hatred of contemporary gross snobbism, forgotten or forgiven it in the past. Because, as she learns from De Quincey, Wordsworth "was abominated and insulted until 1821, when he was fifty-one years of age, and barely tolerated for another ten years, until he was sixty-one," Miss Sitwell for the moment sees him as one of the higher snobs.[37] He appears to her to have been a victim, a victim, she concludes, of the gross snobbism and of the major criticism. This of the Wordsworth who so hastily retracted his adolescent Jacobinism; that "polyhedric Peter" damned by Shelley, a higher snob in comparison with him, in all his sides; who accepted homage from that London "Where small talk dies in agonies"; whose drift from the first was "To be a kind of moral eunuch"; whom the Reviews

who heaped abuse
On Peter while he wrote for freedom,
So soon as in his song they spy
The folly which soothes tyranny,
Praise him, for those who feed 'em.[38]

("Praise him"—W.'s poetry cordially praised in *Blackwood's*, 1817); of whom even Keats in 1818 dared to write: "It may be said that we ought to read our contemporaries. . . . But, for the sake of a few imaginative or domestic passages, are we to be bullied into a certain philosophy engendered in the whims of an Egotist?"; whom Keats disliked for his great-poet snobbism toward him, his conservatism, his flattery of influential persons, his dressing up to dine in a stiff collar "I am sorry that Wordsworth has left a bad impression wherever he visited in town by his egotism, vanity and bigotry"; yet whom Keats continued to consider a literary king; who in 1813 was appointed Stamp-Distributor for Westmoreland by the Regent, in 1815 published his first collective edition, by 1817 was taking part in "immortal dinners"; who became

J.P. for Westmoreland in 1819 and was kindly entertained in 1820 at both universities. All this occurred during a period in which Miss Sitwell considers Wordsworth to have been "abominated and insulted," apparently by the Yellow Press of major criticism. The abomination, as a matter of fact, came from Keats, Shelley, Coleridge and other exponents of the gross snobbism in which, it appears, there are degrees of honour and of sense of calling. In her anxiety to make her case against the Yellow Press fool-proof Miss Sitwell mistook Wordsworth for her kind of snob, which is doing a monstrous injustice both to herself and to the higher snobbism.

Literature, whose authority lay in the special privileges granted it by society, had nothing to fall back on when society, finding literature no longer socially useful, withdrew these privileges. It had no separate confidence, no sense of life as an individual resource: life had been delivered to literature *en masse* in each age as contemporary philosophy. Direct communication with life without the intervention of society had been gradually disappearing since the Elizabethans, so that literature, when it lost caste, could be neither disdainfully indifferent nor openly aggressive; it had to agree and yet not agree, surrender and yet not surrender—to survive by brilliant equivocation. The poet who did not wish to come to blows with the Zeitgeist had no other alternative than to become a snob. The snob is one who defeats circumstances which are against him by not committing himself; one who adopts a strategical position which he does not have to defend because its strategy is so obscure that it is not attacked.

If, then, in spite of everything, literature was to go on at all, it had to be wilfully modern; it had to coincide with its age not by the accidents of personal authorship but by a calculated critical method. Aristotelianism brought up-to-date could therefore settle the problem of contemporary reality for literature better than any new philosophical solution. In revised Aristotelianism, or neo-realism, reality is the final, determining cause and substance that invents all attitudes to it. A poem, as expressing a quality of final reality, is thus little more than automatic effect and the creative mind merely a post-event position of reality. The author of a poem is consequently without personal reality, or responsibility—another important article in snobbist belief.

In such an aesthetic the prevailing system of knowledge becomes the self-knowing Reason. Science is the modernized Self of reality (T. S. Eliot's thomistic God); not Baconian science, which was merely a human method of knowledge, but science as sophisticated substance superior to time and space qualifications, which are the marks of nonsensical, poetical facetiousness in humanity. Advanced contemporary poetry is, as may be verified, facetious, poetical and full of sophisticated nonsense: poetic snobbism is directed chiefly against the humanity, the infantilism, of the poetic mind. And poetry excuses itself by giving itself this ironic title: "The Private Life of the Atom, A Dream Fantasy." Poetry must, that is, be a joke at its own expense, a mature exercise in juvenility. It must no longer live in the time when

> Life went a-maying
> With Nature, Hope and Poesy.[39]

It must rather approach that informed but idiotic bird-wittedness which is the chief charm of the nursery-rhyme. Mr. Eliot's *Waste Land* is the great twentieth-century nursery rhyme. And, like the nursery rhyme, this poetry dispenses with that burden of continuity and sentimental intelligibility implied in an audience. The poet renounces his citizenship in gross humanity and joins that dim social class which lives in the genteel retirement of a few superior critical journals. The only way out for a poet who does not wish to avail himself of the social privileges of his calling, or yet abide in the public maytime reservations still set aside for poets by the modern world out of an inherited sentiment, or yet submerge himself mystically in gross humanity, is to disguise himself as a buffoon; so that his contempt of the complicated snobbisms which paralyse all normal poetic instincts and his own casual cultivation of these instincts may pass for simpleness and he be left to his own devices.

It is easy enough to show historically how such a snobbism has arisen. It is not quite so obvious where the snobs come from, how they are provided. Does the snobbism make the snobs, or the snobs the snobbism? Are the snobs natural snobs or have they been converted to snobbism by contemporary pressure? I think it may be safely ventured that the snobbism was implicit in the Zeitgeist, but that it became an effective snobbism because social development at the same time discharged a class which found this snobbism a useful refuge from historical necessity. The disintegration of the aristocracy left a great many human loose ends who formerly would have been happy as patrons of literature or as gentle amateurs. Deprived of class rank they are now able to keep class rank by the practice of literature. Likewise the farm-boy who formerly achieved gentility by becoming a priest or a scholar now achieves it by practising the higher snobbism in poetry and criticism. The attraction of the higher snobbism as a social aristocracy is naturally felt by the poet who, living in an environment hostile to poetry, sees it also as an intellectual aristocracy holding out to him the promise of freedom from a vulgar age and of consolation in a congenial society. And so have many spirits bold and true been led astray and driven to belie themselves. For less than anything is the higher snobbism an atmosphere congenial to poetry. It is, more than anything, the complete eighteenth century increased in all its manners, most of all increased in Frenchness.

After Frenchness it is increased most of all in Classicism. These arrivistes, by regarding the universe as completed in effect and by covering it with a thin coat of historicity, have achieved an immediate aesthetic absolute. If the end has been reached, then every act is posthumous and has a posthumous finality; and it becomes the function of literature to prolong this finality indefinitely. The age is philosophically conclusion on the brink of conclusion. The serenity of classicism has always derived from an underlying historical posthumousness, as the turbulence of romanticism from an underlying pre-natalism.

Only one thing stands in the way of perfect posthumousness, a slow and irregular population-mass which is always arriving late, and so interfering with the higher snobbism's complete view of finality, even forcing the higher snobbism to make a few mistakes in calculation. If everything could be classically classified as science, the literary expression of finality would be simple enough, for science is so far advanced into itself that it is already in its literary stage. But unfortunately certain elements of contemporary life, such as politics, remain backward and stubbornly human. It is just here that the higher snobbism is likely to commit regrettable errors of judgment, being equipped to interpret nothing but finality, and to be wholly unable to make an intelligent choice between one relative fact and another—between, say, Communism and Fascism. Yet for the most part, the contemporary and snob succeeds in keeping himself away from the population-mass, which is not the Zeitgeist but the dregs of many Zeitgeists; from anything, in fact, which looks like sentimental rescue-work of the floating wreckage of time. As far as possible he wants to rid himself of the pathetic errors of personality and make the creative operation a pure critical reflex, free of error. Now nothing can be free of error unless it is entirely negative; *Ulysses* is in this way a great snob-work because it is a synthesis of as many negative forces as could be assembled in a given time-limit. In poetic form the result of removing subjective determination is a minimum of originality and a maximum of freakishness. A great quantity of false aesthetic material may thus be disposed of and the values generally used to animate such material permanently discredited. But when this snobbism, this fear of error, has done its work, what is left? Does there remain any ground for independent creative activity, for a positive poetic life? In the modernized quantitative cosmos of the Western mind, in this blight of perfection, where is there room for new errors? There is room for nothing but an empty philosophical absolute, whose hypothetical reality the negative, qualitative cosmos of criticism derives from the quantitative cosmos.

This is the dreary situation which the higher snobbism has brought about by expelling error from art. For with error went works in the sense of personal authorship, since works were imperfect because of authorship; and for works criticism had therefore to substitute philosophy. Criticism is left with nothing to talk about but its prejudices; and so it becomes more dogmatic, more formalistic, more obscure and more free from error from day to day. Even the poetry written by the higher snobbism can only be, by its very perfection, a form of criticism composed by the whole snobbist machine, a philosophical but not an aesthetic act. And even as criticism it must fail because it borrows its aesthetic terms from philosophy, the logical enemy of any creative principle, since it is opposed to any *really* real absolute. Philosophy is the religion that fills the critical senses with illusions of purified reality when ordinary human reality is, for one reason or another, under a cloud. It is therefore the principal consolation of the contemporary and snob and allies him with that long and aristocratic line of literary defeatists who have always protected poetry from the facts and errors of life by allowing criticism to substitute poetics for persons. What the higher snobbism wants above all things is consistency. Theoretically it can get consistency by conforming to the Zeitgeist, which has in this age so separated itself from the human population-mass and advanced so far beyond it that it is free of those imperfections which spring up in any system when it begins to be humanly assimilated. Never, in fact, has philosophical reality (for the Zeitgeist, or contemporary reality, is only philosophical reality) been further removed than at present from human reality, which for this reason seems more inconsistent than ever. The more systematic philosophical reality becomes, the greater the breach between it and human reality; the more inconsistent, in fact, it becomes itself. The illusion of consistency in philosophical reality is due to its inhumanity, and its perfection is merely a proof of its irrelevance. To be humanly consistent and philosophically consistent in a single stroke one would have to conform to neither human nor philosophical reality; one would have to be, in other words, an irregular genius capable of an act of creative consistency from which both realities could be simultaneously derived. This would mean the brutal victory of the person over numbers and their abstraction. But the higher snobbism spurns victory; it considers the person a sentimental vulgarity; and it does not want to have anything to do with numbers except through the mediation of philosophy, which deals only in perfected social abstractions of incomplete, sluggish humanity. And here it rests.

The person in poetry began to lose standing because the poetic faculty came to be identified with a set of poetical sensations which may be summarized as sentimentality. So much of the private personal data involved in the making of poetry had been vulgarized and divulged by the influx of confused and high-strung democratic elements, that the gentlemen of poetry disclaimed the poetic faculty in order to avoid writing unladylike poetry: the ribaldry of Eliot, Cummings and Joyce are instances of this conscientious effort on the part of gentlemen-authors to avoid the temptations to sentimentality inherent in the poetic faculty; this effort, that is, to be ladies. Suppressed ribaldry in gentlemen-authors, as in Miss Marianne Moore and Miss Edith Sitwell, generally means that the temptations to sentimentality have been yielded to, though without vulgarity: in Miss Moore's poetry by putting sentimental poetic subjects under a cold shower of prose-language and prose-technique, in Miss Sitwell's by abducting sentimentality to that strange still-life land of metallic fruits and decorous kitchen-gardens in which it would be difficult for anything to be vulgar.

But not only did poetry reach a stage where it was impossible to write with taste without observing a large number of critical taboos; the language of criticism itself had become so vulgarized that its dearest, most cherished property rights in its key-words, such as Imagination, Beauty, Truth, Feeling, became meaningless. Criticism had therefore to withdraw itself from this vulgarized poetry and this vulgarized language of criticism, which had originally been taken over from philosophy. Gentleman-criticism and gentleman-poetry now worked hand in hand, criticism refreshing itself once more in the fount of philosophy, poetry learning at the feet of criticism a new code of thoroughly censored behaviour by which it became an impeccable though obscure intellectual observance. The fount of philosophy at which criticism refreshed itself was the Zeitgeist, the philosophical aggregate of the age. But the Zeitgeist is never an exact historical equivalent of the age, in some ages less so than in others; the less so as knowledge-material becomes more and more systematized. The Zeitgeist of the early nineteenth century was an approximate historical equivalent of its age because contemporary knowledge-material was disorganized and therefore humanly realistic. There was one whole fixed Zeitgeist throughout the Middle Ages because of epistemological over-organization and rigidity; the geographical succession of Renaissance Zeitgeists and their human relevance was due to the breakdown of this very rigidity. There is as much difference between the human relevance of the present Zeitgeist and that of the Platonic Zeitgeist as between the distance of the *Phaedrus*, let us say, from the average person of 360 B.C. and the distance of the Theory of Relativity from the average person of 1927.

The present Zeitgeist is, indeed, a Renaissance Zeitgeist with an abnormally low degree of human relevance as a philosophical aggregate. Nor would it be pertinent to object that this cannot be so, since philosophy as such has disappeared. Philosophy seems to have disappeared only because knowledge has become more philosophical, more systematized: the Zeitgeist is nearly entirely without human relevance. Its irrelevance, in fact, means that in a human sense it is without system, that it has a forced systematism to disguise its internal inconsistency. Actually any system of knowledge at a given moment has as much inconsistency as there is inconsistency in humanity at that moment; which is just why a *system* of knowledge is a philosophical tyranny and a historical falsehood. If, however, the *Phaedrus* and the Theory of Relativity were treated as independent human acts, consistent in themselves but of human inconsistency, then they could exercise no more tyranny than could a fine, elaborate poem. Instead, because they are presented as systems, neither Platonism nor modern science ever become effectively real, as a poem can, but merely literary, as Platonism survives in vague Truth-and-Beauty terminology, and as science, which becomes literary very quickly, reaches humanity in electrical devices, cancer cures and radio-entertainments, which are purely literary manifestations of science.

What, then, is the code which contemporary criticism, bathing in the perennial and ever-changing fount of philosophy, the Zeitgeist, delivers for the benefit of that impeccable though obscure intellectual observance? Can it be that the social backing of contemporary poetic gentlemanliness is only, after all, a gloomy medley of scholastic anthropology, spaded Freudianism, Baroque Baedeckerism, sentimental anti-quarianism, slum-and-boudoir philology, mystical Bradleyanism, tortoise-shell spectacled natural history, topee'd comparative religion and Arrow-collared Aristotelianism?—Aristotelianism first and last, because it is the most dogmatic, tight-laced ethical system ever devised outside of a tribal religion, and without the human passion and error of a religion, a literary substitute for Christian asceticism; and because romanticizations of it have never reached the vulgar population-mass, as with Platonism?

As criticism has gone so far beyond erratic humanity and the perceptive intelligence into pure, automatic Being and Knowing, it is natural that the first article of that obscure intellectual observance should be a renunciation of pathetic personality, a profession of lack of faith in self and of distrust in the human mind. To this extreme was it necessary to go to justify the expulsion of those words, subjects, attitudes and sensations which had fallen into literary disrepute. Granted the provocation, in what way, however, is the poetic faculty to be carried safely through a Zeitgeist which not only denies the reality of poetry but with which criticism allies itself as well in denying the reality of the poet? Obviously the poetic faculty cannot get through the Zeitgeist unless some poet or other carries it through on his back. But can he carry it through if he makes a formal deposition of disbelief in the human mind? Can he afford to disregard the Zeitgeist and carry the poetic faculty through without making such a deposition, when to withhold it means social disgrace, that is, critical ostracism? Can he behave in a way not becoming to the Zeitgeist and get through the Zeitgeist? Can he get through at all if he does behave in a becoming way? A poet deficient in the poetic faculty may make as noble a deposition of distrust in the human mind as one abundantly supplied with it. Perhaps the only way to get through the Zeitgeist is to acknowledge it and let it hurry on, leaving the poetic faculty behind to make continuous refutations of poetic Adventism. To help pass away the time, while this is happening, the poet with the poetic faculty strapped on his back may play the buffoon, call criticism "nuncle" and cajole it into a historical accuracy in the dating of poetry, pointing out, with his bladder-stick, that it must allow biographical corrections of the Zeitgeist, as man is permitted to improve on Time, since if Time were left to itself there would be no to-morrow.

Note

The preceding essay is a long-term view of the relations of the poet with the world he lives in. The following essay is a short-term view of a single generation of poetry by itself and of its internal problems and tendencies. No close correlation has therefore been made between them, and none should be; although they will be found to agree in their general implications.

2
T. E. Hulme, the New Barbarism, and Gertrude Stein

I

The most obvious thing about contemporary poetry is that it is "difficult." It first of all appears difficult in the reading; so great a distance separates the contemporary poet from the contemporary reader that the only contemporary reader possible seems to be the poet himself. It then appears that the difficulty is perhaps in the writing rather than in the reading. The reader's difficulties are a reflection of those which the contemporary poet has to face if he wishes to write as a contemporary—to be included in the generation to which, by birth and personal sympathy, he historically belongs. They determine the external character of the text because they belong to its internal character.[1]

Now in general date or time is an arbitrary convenience adopted to distinguish in the memory one day, one hour from the other. To the reader, the poet, or the night-watchman it is simply an artificial system of classification. We do not feel different on waking up to-day, because to-day is to-day, from what we felt on waking up yesterday. We have to make the mental effort of registering in our waking consciousness that to-day is to-day; it is indeed this mental effort that increases our age. No one really feels older than he felt yesterday; second-childhood, for instance, is merely the cessation of the mental effort required to mark down sunrise and sunset as time.

As the poet, if a true poet, is one by nature and not by effort, he must be seen as writing as unconsciously (in regard to time, at any rate) as his ordinary reader lives. The relation of his poetry to Poetry and to the time in which it is written is the problem of criticism; and if this problem enters into the actual writing of his poetry it must do so by being superimposed upon it. A new and even alien element is in this case added to his poetry—

the historical effort. His reader must not only make the effort demanded by the difference between his own way of existing unconsciously and the poet's way of existing unconsciously—he must not only consciously compare his own unconsciousness with the poet's unconsciousness; he must make the same historical effort that the poet makes. He must make the poet's creative difficulties his own critical difficulties. This is why, in a generation of poetry so significantly marked by such a historical effort, the plain reader is inclined to be more sympathetic with the poetry of a past period than with that of his own period: by belonging to the past, past poetry makes the historical effort for him.

If contemporary poetry is for various reasons written with this effort, there is no escape for the reader but to make the effort himself; otherwise he must be content to wait until contemporary poetry has become history, until, presumably, his generation is dead. Or, if he has sufficient receptivity and historical awareness of the present, he need not make a special effort in his reading. He is a contemporary reader before he reads. He is armed with his criticism.

Indeed, in some ways it seems more reasonable for the reader to make the historical effort than for the poet, as it is more a part of the consuming side of poetry than of the creative side. But the facts are otherwise. Poetry has been the victim of increasing pressure and isolation. It has been obliged to specialize and over-specialize in itself. It has been narrowed down by the specialization of human time-activities to a point where it seems only another human time-activity, where it becomes, in other words, an art in the most formal interpretation of the word. The poet therefore has forced upon him the whole burden of the criticism of poetry. He has forced upon him a historical consciousness far more acute than that, say, of the travelling bard of the *Beowulf* period or of the professional poet of an imperially or religiously phrased society. Such poets merely met certain demands laid upon them by an environment in which they were generously included. The modernist poet has no such easy social adjustment to make: it is doubtful whether he is included at all in the complicated social pattern. As a result he is more at the service of the public situation of poetry, which is a perilous one, than of his private poetic endowments. He may, in a few rare cases, by a sort of historical absent-mindedness, happen to write by pure nature, without historical or professional effort. But on the whole it is probable that he will be affected, and forgivably affected, by the pressure and influence of a commercial society on poetry. He will be too conscious of the forced professionalization of poetry to resist the temptation to justify it professionally. But if he admits that it is only one of the numerous time-activities of its period, an activity parallel to music or painting, as other time-activities, or to radiology, aerostatics, the cinema, modern tennis or morbid psychology, he must see it in its contemporary setting as a very small patch on the time-chart, a bare dot. The only way that this dot, this poetry-patch, can be given depth is by being given historical depth. Then its local reality and significance can be made to lie not so much in its general importance as an expression of this particular period or age (for obviously as an expression of this age it is no more than a dot on a hysterically overcrowded chart) as in its particular importance in the general tradition of poetry.

The tradition of poetry, or, we had better now say, the tradition of the *art* of poetry, is therefore the formal organization which the modernist poet finds himself serving as an affiliated member. He must not only, if he accepts this view of the situation of poetry (whether out of conviction or necessity), have a personal capacity for poetry—this is merely his apprenticeship-certificate. He must have beyond this a master's sense of the historical experience of poetry, of its functions, its usefulness, its present fitness and possibilities. He must have a science of the "values" of poetry; a scale of good and bad or true and false or lasting and ephemeral; a theory of a tradition of poetry in which successive period-poetries are subjected to historical judgment either favourably or unfavourably, and in which his own period-poetry is carefully adjusted to satisfy the values which the tradition is believed to have evolved. Furthermore, since this tradition is supposed to represent a logical historical development, its values, if observed, are considered sufficient to produce the proper poetic expression of the age. The adjustments which the poet has to make are no longer direct, unconscious adjustments to his social environment, but critical adjustments to a special tradition: his contact with his own period is indirect, through the past, the past seen narrowly as the literature of the past narrowing down to the literature, more particularly the poetry, of the present.

So it comes about that the modernist poet tends to have an exaggerated, even an abnormal preoccupation with criticism: largely forced upon him, as has been noted, by the defensive position into which poetry is put by modern life. A professional conscience dawns on the poet; as when the prestige of any organization is curtailed—of the army, or the navy, for example—a greater internal discipline, a stricter morality and a more careful evaluation of tactics result. The organization becomes self-critical, severe, sophisticated; strenuously up-to-date and of its generation; the critic of itself in the past. In poetry the negative side of this discipline shows itself in the avoidance of all the wrongly conceived habits of the past. Poetry becomes so educated in itself that it knows or seems to know at last how it should be written and written at the very moment. The more its tradition is limited and purified of elements like religion, science, psychology, philosophy or sociology, which once existed in it as loose sentiments, the more technically expert in them it grows; and in itself, by imitative sympathy. It looks indeed as if the poetry of the period could be written by historical effort alone; as if poetry has become so civilized, so all-aware, that in its most advanced stage it is on the brink of a new primitive stage. It seems about to begin again as from the beginning but drawing on the experience of its tradition.

In practice, however, this new stage is only implied, not realized, in contemporary poetry. True, there is more experimenting and greater strictness in the construction of the poem, and a greater consciousness of what a poem should not be. But so far this consciousness has remained a negative influence: it is a professional, critical self-consciousness, not a creative one. And how should it be creative? Creative self-consciousness is a contradiction in terms; for it is clear that poets do not begin to write by effort but by nature. It might seem, however, that such an atmosphere, if it did not actually produce poets, would at least make it easier for those who were poets by nature to write well, by removing all temptations to write badly, and by creating a feeling of tolerance toward a possible new poetry. But it is if anything more difficult than usual to write either well or badly in an atmosphere charged with discussion and self-consciousness about the "values" of poetry and about how poetry should be written in conformity with the period. Such an atmosphere forces the historical effort upon the poet. It confounds the problems of criticism with the problems of writing. It hampers the poet with the poetry of all poets who have ever written, who may be writing at the moment, or who will ever write. It invents—and this is the most serious drawback—a group poetic mind which is at the elbow of the individual poet whenever he engages in composition. This contemporary climate is as much responsible for the "difficulty" of modernist poetry as the fact that well-written poetry is always difficult and that the criticism responsible for this climate demands that contemporary poetry should be well written. So the reasons why there should be a new poetry prove to be the very ones why there is not a new poetry but only a disturbed, a self-critical, a tightly written, a strongly corrective poetry; why we shall probably find ourselves to have had, after the novelties have been absorbed by tradition, not a new age of poetry, in which new resources have been opened up for the poetic mind, but merely another generation of poets, a generation that has already begun to pass.

For however opposed this generation may have been to certain tendencies in the poetic tradition, it has been bound over from the very beginning to the idea of a tradition, and of a correct tradition. The passion for correctness has led it to many strange caprices; to an admiration for the eighteenth century in English poetry as the most correct literary period of modern times; to a bias in favour of the most foppishly correct classical writers; to such odd niceties and pains and punctilios that it is not extravagant to suggest to the contemporary reader that the poetry peculiar to his generation is perhaps the most correct poetry that has ever been written in the English language. So intense has this process been, so thorough and hurried at the same time, that it has made poetry a narrower time-activity from within than it has been made, even, from without. The generation is already over before its time, having counted itself out and swallowed itself up by its very efficiency—a true "lost generation,"[2] as Gertrude Stein has called it and as it is fond of calling itself. Already its most correct writer, T. S. Eliot, has become a classic over the heads of the plain reader. The plain reader who would now first read the poetry of his time must read it as already passed into tradition. Although he will find a high degree of application necessary for the actual word-by-word reading of the various works, he is spared that more elaborate effort of criticism which deals with works as potential classics. The whole problem of taste, that is, has been taken care of for him by the poets themselves, who have written their poems with such precision and far-sightedness that "acceptance" as such has been made superfluous. Creation and critical judgment being made one act, a work has no future history with readers; it is ended when it is ended.

In practice, then, there is no such thing as a new poetry; only a short and very concentrated period, already nearly over, of carefully disciplined and self-conscious poetry. It is almost just to say that at the present moment there is no poetry but rather an embarrassing pause after an arduous and erudite stock-taking. The next stage is not clear. But it is not impossible that when the embarrassment has passed there will be a resumption of less foppish, less strained, more critically unconscious poetic methods of writing, purified, however, by the period of historical effort behind it. At any rate for the time being we have nothing better than this pause and in it an opportunity of understanding what has taken place. We might almost say that poetry temporarily turned into philosophy, entangled itself in many introspective absurdities that had nothing to do with poetry, became pretentiously scholastic and dogmatic in its theory; but that all this was perhaps unfortunately necessary before a position could be reached in which poetry might be normal without being vulgar, and deal naturally with truth without being trite.

Such an embarrassed lull having fallen in poetry, the result of minute searching and conscientiousness, the abstract nature of poetry eventually becomes more important to the poet than the immediate personal workings of poetry in him. His introspectiveness, which up to a certain technical point might make his poetry clearer and more careful, when carried beyond this point makes the writing of poetry altogether impossible by turning it into a pursuit of theory and the poet into a scientific investigator. So the philosophical phase of poetic modernism is a laboratory phase, a complex interrelation of metaphysics and psychology blighting the creative processes wherever they become involved in it. This can be well-illustrated by comparing the highly organized nature of T. S. Eliot's criticism in its present stage with the gradual disintegration of his poetry since the *Waste Land*.[3] The absolute sense of authorship has been lost and the poet finds himself counting only as he can be related to the historical period to which he accidentally belongs. The time-element is made the law of composition and any work which cannot be readily interpreted in terms of its period-significance cannot be said to have any critical value—which at the moment is the one admissible value by which poetry can become current. The only good in this critical obsession is that, while it may cause many temporary extravagances and suppressions, by stirring up a historical consciousness of poetry it may make the world in general more conscious of poetry in a specialized sense and more intimate with its processes. In the end the emphasis on up-to-dateness and the time-element in poetry may only mean a greater concentration in both the reader and the poet on poetry as an ever immediate reality confirmed afresh and independently in each new work rather than as a continuously sustained tradition: confirmed personally rather than professionally.

II

There are discoverable reasons why the time-element came to have such importance in contemporary poetry and criticism. Literature in the past had been forced to recognize barbaric definitions of time which might be foreign to the nature of literature but were imposed by local convenience: the poet accepted authorized "ideas" of God or Immortality or State and invented within these limits. He used, that is, the formal human language of his time. The language and the time were barbaric because they were gross dogmatic conventions resulting from the fear-inspired consolidation of humanity. Humanity is a consolidation against the terror of numbers, each unknown, which would reign if humanity were not consolidated as humanity. When humanity is so consolidated it becomes a stabilized and known mass, a weapon against any non-human unknown. Of the various ways in which humanity may be consolidated—by some symbol of individual similarity, whether of religious beliefs or government, or by the observance of common social taboos—

contemporaneousness, the idea of the numbers sharing in one time, is the most unifying sentiment. Poetry was obliged to acquiesce in this sentiment because language is the most tangible sign of local uniformity: the poet had to accept his medium from humanity at large, to allow it, indeed, to invent his medium for him. If organic changes took place in the language, they were not caused by any inventive caprice in him or because he shifted, and his medium with him, in adjusting himself to time. Humanity shifted, as a whole, perhaps, in making some slight adjustment within itself, and language with it; and this might be called a manifestation of barbaric time. But the poet had no particular consciousness or responsibility of time. He was in this respect free of the historical effort which is forced on the present-day poet. The historical effort was assigned to all as a mass and to none in particular.

The barbaric tendency expresses itself in mass, the civilized tendency in specialization. When the necessity for consolidated mass passes, mass breaks up into smaller units; it substitutes civilization for consolidation. The tendency to consolidate does not necessarily, however, antedate the tendency to specialize. The barbaric tendency might reasonably be inculcated in an individualistic society, out of common fear and compulsion. At all events, European barbarism comes finally to be replaced by humanism: humanity viewed as a quality in the individual rather than in the mass—as personality. Instead of one gross composite time we have as many times going on at once as there are individual expressions of dissimilar personality going on at once. Or, to look at it differently, time has become so relative that the individual need not be necessarily conscious of it. The poet in a barbaric period is free from historical effort because time is absolute, he has no power over it; and he is free from historical effort in a civilized period because time is so strictly personal a measurement that he has complete power over it.

The disintegrating effect of civilization is not only felt in the development of personality. As the abstract idea of humanity is broken up into concrete personal existences and the conception of time changes accordingly, so the categories developed by barbarism to express the underlying principle of the solidarity of humanity are now used to express the non-cohesiveness of humanity. The language that once served the conformity of human interests now serves their diversity. Each category becomes specialized into a study of itself and each discovers, in terms appropriate to it, its own theory of the relativity of time. Each category becomes a separate time-activity. In a barbaric society religion does not occupy one mental compartment, philosophy another, science another, painting another, poetry another, and so on. But religion is everything and everything is religion, philosophy is everything and everything is philosophy, and so on. In a civilized society religion is a sentiment, philosophy a speculation, science a pursuit of knowledge, painting and poetry arts.

The arts have the most difficult problem to face in a specializing civilization because when converted into separate activities they retain something of their original force. They continue to have to do principally with *being* and *making* and being and making is everything and everything is being and making. When, however, they try to treat themselves as specialized departments of *study* and at the same time to continue to be the subjects of their study, to remain the kind of activity they have been from the beginning, an impossibility is struck upon. And yet this impossibility is the basis of the civilized conception of such activities as arts, *art* being apparently a term applied to intellectual activities which are something more than studies of themselves.

In an art, it seems, two powers are concerned, the original power which is the subject of the art—the being and making—and the power to study this power; both powers being presumably one and the same. In an ordinary category like science, where there is nothing but the study, all that is involved is a laborious registering of changes which are continually taking place in the study. The study is the minute observation of the tradition and the deriving from this observation of the time or *pace* which is peculiar to this tradition. Religion is such an observation of a tradition, a sensitive registering of the changes which observation itself brings about in the study.

But in an art, in poetry let us say, there is the study, in which changes are always taking place (else there could be no study, for this is the meaning of study, which is not repetition), and there is the other power, which is pure from the beginning and in which no changes can take place without the destruction of the art as a category. Science, though a single tradition, is a different thing in Einstein's time from what it was in Archimedes' time; and the tradition permits of its being this radically different thing. Poetry, however, is not a different thing in T. S. Eliot's time from what it was in Euripides' time; if it were, neither Euripides nor Eliot could be defined as poets and the tradition would be non-existent. How, then, is the poetic tradition to move in time and yet poetry itself to remain unchanged; and how is this further impossibility to be overcome, that the study, which is the continuousness of the tradition, or the object of the art, cannot go on at the same time as the being and making which are the subject of the art?

Up to a certain stage in its history as a civilized category, poetry escapes from these impossibilities and maintains itself as an art by formally dividing itself into a composing half and a studying half, the former limited to workmanship, the latter to criticism. The poet as a workman being naturally free from the time-sense and the historical effort, criticism devotes itself to the cultivation of a poetic time-sense and to its imposition on the poet. Poetry has a relative civilized time, then, only while the pressure of criticism on the workman-poet is so light that he has his own relative time and not that of poetry as a whole. It is when poetry is forced to over-specialize and professionalize itself as a category and workmanship and criticism are narrowed down to a single process, that the falsity of the categorization of poetry either in a barbaric or civilized sense becomes plain. For when this happens poetry must get its consolidated time-sense from criticism rather than from workmanship: workmanship is as various and contradictory as the number of workmen. What Mr. Eliot calls "the invalidation of that ancient classification,"[4] the disappearance, that is, of the distinction between *critical* and *creative*, is in reality the domination of creation by criticism. If creation were to dominate criticism, criticism would disappear. While criticism and creation exist side by side with only a loose partnership between them, creation is for the most part carefree, it has a general but not disturbing intelligence of the tradition of poetry and tolerates criticism as a harmless and even an occasionally useful parasite. Underneath the bustle and clutter of historical interpretations, underneath the disguise of a category—poetry can be free to be what it has always been, an entity which can lend itself to the absolute entirety of barbaric humanity or to the relative entirety of civilized personality, but which remains fundamentally independent of and unaffected by historical changes; its purpose being not to express history, humanity or personality, but itself.

When poetry reaches the stage in its history as a civilized category where criticism, or the studying-half, dominates the workmanship-half, and the unsuitability of poetry as a specialized art makes both criticism and workmanship very difficult, it is actually in danger of being destroyed as a tradition unless some time-sense is introduced into it, by no matter how artificial an effort. No one seems to realize that the destruction of poetry as a tradition would not destroy poetry itself. Those who are not poets do not, because to see poetry as such an independent force requires that one should be a poet. And those who are poets are tempted to encourage the idea of the traditional professionality of poetry because it confers a group-dignity and power that protects their personal sensitiveness. Consequently there is no debate about the necessity of preserving the tradition; and it is criticism which assumes responsibility for the collective unity of the art of poetry.

The time-sense by which such unity can be consciously maintained must be, it is evident, a mass, or barbaric, time-sense and not a personalized, or civilized, one. Thus when all other categories, particularly those generally classified as scientific, are developing minutely relative time-senses, poetry (and painting as well) attempts to stabilize itself by evoking an absolute time-sense. This new intellectual barbarism must, of course, differ from a natural historical barbarism. In the latter, mass-time and mass-humanity are real and automatically fixed and absolute, so that the poet is free of any conscious effort to construe his time. In the former there is no mass-time or mass-humanity, time and humanity are personal sentimentalities; so that the concept of absoluteness by which poetry as a whole may have some historical coherence must first be consciously postulated before the poet can claim any meaning for his work. In consequence the meaning and the making of a poem become two separate elements. Meaning is the substance of criticism, and a general, common problem. Making in its most limited sense is the substance of workmanship and tends, as in most modernist poetry, to grow more and more particularized and technical. Criticism now actually precedes workmanship.

To support such a theory of barbaric absoluteness poetry must ally itself with a special metaphysic of poetry. It must even, in self-defence, believe that the new barbarism is a natural and not a forced stage in the tradition, must even believe that, because a conscious stage, it is a superior, in fact a final one. It must make the present period not so much the next one of a series as a resume of periods. Its obligatory concern with the general meanings of poetry and the maintenance of a formal metaphysic of poetry tempt it to assume the position formerly belonging to philosophy. In defining the poetic absolute a hierarchy or graduated order of values is established, converting poetry into a dogmatic science pledged to the refinement of these values. The personal creative side of poetry is overshadowed by the professional traditional side.

The effect of this scientific attitude may eventually be to give the poem itself greater distinctness; in contemporary poetry there have been many efforts to present the poem as a thing in itself, a definite object produced by a conscientious craftsman. Its general immediate influence has been to put an unnatural burden of faultlessness on the poem. The modernist poem probably suffers more than it benefits from the attention which contemporary criticism grants it. If on the one hand it has acquired a new sort of conspicuousness, it has been forced, on the other hand, to have a greater regularity than would otherwise have been necessary.

An absolute which shall give the poem a regularity more certain than the accidental regularity that it has in a civilized, more relatively stated aspect of the tradition can at present be only an absolute in theory—it begins as an idea not a fact. It cannot be a virtual absolute because, however regular the poem itself should be if the poet adheres to this theory, the necessity of adhering to a theory remains an ineradicable flaw. It is possible and interesting to observe that at such and such a historic period an absolute conception of humanity, time and art prevailed and that a peculiarly fixed kind of perfection in art, as in Egyptian art, developed from this conception. Such a general observation is history; if particularly applied, as to poetry, it is criticism. But if criticism is made something more than observation, if it develops such a preference for the barbaric absolute, say, that it attempts to give this to poetry artificially, by historical effort, then it is creating not poetry but history. Critically conceived poetry at the present time is historical rather than poetic. Historical inventiveness of this kind is, as we shall see, fundamentally Bergsonian.[5] It is as if all individual consciousnesses were expected to be able at will to submerge themselves completely in a single race-consciousness and for a protracted period evolve with great intensity and at great strides, without variation, digression or error. All separate poetic faculties, that is, are supposed to merge into a single professional group-faculty of which each poet is separately possessed. The poetic production as a whole, where such an effort is made, would have great theoretical simplicity because criticism had conceived and directed it as a whole; but equally, great practical complexity, since individual poetic faculties cannot submerge themselves at will in an absolute faculty except by such intricacies of theory as complicate the whole the more theoretically simple it is.

It is not surprising, therefore, that poetry has for the moment assumed the position formerly occupied by philosophy. Philosophy is pure history and pure criticism. It observes, and from its observations it creates something which pretends to be neither actual history nor actual poetry. Its purpose is to generalize from particulars and to simplify its generalities with the idea of discovering a code of perfection. The end of all philosophies, however much they have seemed to contradict one another, has been to define the absolute. Committed to a belief in the reality of the generalities by which they arrived at this absolute, they have, moreover, been bound to minimize the reality of variation, digression or error. *Caprice* is never more than a foot-note subject in any philosophy; its conclusions must obviously be only those which humanity can arrive at as a single-minded, barbaric whole. This systematic conformity of pure philosophy is, described in historical language, classicism.

So it has happened that when the absolutist conception of humanity was succeeded by the relativist conception of personality (humanism), pure philosophy disappeared. Since the Renaissance caprice has governed the forms which human thought and conduct have taken; and caprice is romanticism. Not only this, but thought and conduct have found a common ground in which they are united and of equal potency—Imagination; and Imagination is romanticism. In classicism the distinctions between thought and conduct are strictly drawn, and philosophy must observe these distinctions in order to protect the idea of perfection: once they are allowed to disappear, imperfection or error or caprice is admitted as a fundamental generality. Since the Renaissance, then, formal philosophy has grown more and more feeble, as Time, the generality capable of most uniformity, has grown more and more diversified and relative. Philosophy, when narrowed down by the large-scale diversification of civilized humanity into a minor category or time-activity, could obviously not develop itself as such, could not acquiesce in its own relativity without contradicting itself.

The only chance of reviving its old authority was, if some category like poetry, which originally had first-class, general significance in a barbaric order, should in being civilized be weakened as a category; should consequently need assistance in re-establishing its professional standing. In an individualized time-combination, poetry or any previously standardized tradition becomes, up to a certain point, more and more non-professional. Then this very non-professionalism itself is loosely professionalized. We have stereotyped individuality instead of stereotyped uniformity, or the standardization of specialization. It is in such circumstances that poetry feels tempted to take specialization literally and to dignify itself by turning its haphazard professionalism into a formal, authoritative professionalism. It accepts the specialized denomination art, but within the limits set by this denomination it enforces its own peculiar generalities—generalities which imply a system of the absolute and therefore the entire machinery and vocabulary of "pure" philosophy.

III

The new poetic barbarism could be felt in poetry in a disorganized way as an intellectual necessity and even conscientiously carried out as a programme by individual poets, though in a still more disorganized way. But it was important that it should have its philosopher and that he should be, besides, a person disappointed in the course taken by philosophy since the Renaissance—in the decline of "pure" philosophy. The pressure exerted on poetry to interpret itself by a conscious historical effort as a coherent tradition drove it to organize itself temporally. Its sole contemporary object became an expression of the age which would not only justify itself professionally but redefine time for it in an absolute way. Thus a hunger was created in the generation on which the pressure fell for some doctrinaire statement of this philosophization of poetry, and a readiness to make a modern Aristotle of the person who could do something toward satisfying the hunger. Such a person was provided in the late T. E. Hulme, who died before he had developed a well-defined system of aesthetics, but who left enough fragments to be accepted by a generation starved for respectable philosophico-literary dogma.[6] It is significant that his philosophy was founded on a view of the absolute which was more religious than philosophical, and more proper to art than to religion. In searching for a way to purify philosophy, he could find nothing better than the need which art—painting or sculpture or poetry—had to be philosophically organized and corrected. All his statements about the nature of pure philosophy will be found to apply more accurately to art than to philosophy.

Hulme's absolute was a strictly barbaric concept: anti-humanism, anti-Renaissance, anti-civilization. In his division of reality into its prime zones or categories he derided any idea of relativity among them. His absolute implied what he called a principle of discontinuity, and it is amusing to find that he named these categories in such a way that no communication could seem plausible between them. They were the *inorganic* world, the *organic* world and the world of *religious* and *ethical* values. It is clear how he arrived at them. For they are the categories into which evolutionary time naturally falls if progressive historical continuity is assumed: first the world of apparently final, static, unformulated matter, then that of growing, or changing matter (the human world), then the world of forms created by this growth—the world, we might say, of formulated matter, really final and static. Now let these categories stand but remove the conception of time in process which invented them and we have the same categories, their definition unchanged, but *discontinuous*. All objectionable notions of time and relativity will then appear to have proceeded from the second category. In the first is a seeming absolute, the brutal absolute of mere primitiveness, in the third is a true absolute possessing all those attributes by cultivation which in the first belong by crudeness. Time is absolute in the first because it is so completely absent as to be uniform. In the third it is absolute because the uniformity is aesthetic and creates the absoluteness of time. The two complementary factors in this creation are the exercise and the submission of the will. Therefore this third category, which is really the field of aesthetics, is called the world of religious and ethical values. The second is not even properly speaking a category, it is the whole imperfect and vacillating human intelligence, a kind of freak of nature, which has the vanity to attempt to find in itself a subjective mock-Divine. Nor is the first category, properly speaking, a category, but only a rough unrealized statement of the third. Only one true general category does, in fact, exist, the single barbaric absolute in which religion, ethics, and art combine to objectify and fix the temporal phases through which the human intelligence, out of imperfection and caprice, passes.

Such a dogmatic interpretation of history—(I have only extended Hulme's fundamental propositions)—for it is an interpretation of history although it does not adopt the conventionally historical view—can obviously be of great value to a particular tradition which, like poetry, has been placed in a position of self-defence and made to feel the need of systematizing itself. It can be especially valuable because, by discrediting the idea of history as necessary continuity of time in which all human personalities or groups of personalities share variously and freely, and by making it a discontinuous principle, it suggests that there is an inevitable order in it to which the human intelligence may be held generally responsible. The productions of an age cannot answer for themselves by declaring "We are these several productions and the age exists through our variety and contemporaneity." They are, on the contrary, incidental to the age and a corroboration of it. The age is not an expression of the relativity of the various activities going on in it, but these activities express it and their relativity is due to its absoluteness; it is not a short period or piece of time but all time—the world indeed of religious and ethical values—attested to and worshipped by a number of individual times. It is a curious fact that whenever such barbaric ideology as this has prevailed the age has been so compact that it has not had "periods." It has appeared final and eternal and prolonged itself artificially and even destroyed itself by prolonging itself. Mediaevalism, for example, was a protracted absolute and unvaried throughout by minor periods or by any relative sense of time.

Once poetry through its criticism becomes aware that the personal authority of the poet in a relative, civilized time-scheme is reduced to the small accidental share he has in it, then such a view of time as a belief in an absolute affords must naturally appeal to poets as a conscious contemporary body. It is beside the point that such a body would be an artificial one, that poetry considered as a specialized activity reduces to the poet, not to the co-ordinated production of poets (while science does not reduce to the scientist). The fact is that the appearance of inevitable co-ordination is forced upon poetry and that it seems to lose authority unless it imposes co-ordination. Poetry cannot be left to its fate with the poet, whose proportionate authority is now as infinitesimal as the constituents of the atom. The only way to give poetry formal authority is through some philosophical system like the one that Hulme roughly suggested.

Hulme's ideas have by now been absorbed by sensitive contemporary criticism and indeed inspire, however remotely, most contemporary poetry consciously written as part of a co-ordinated period-production: "he appears as the forerunner of a new attitude of mind, which should be the twentieth-century mind," was the *New Criterion*'s summary of his significance.[7] Hulme himself wrote a few poems, and it is interesting that they all come vaguely under the period-classification popular in his time: Imagism. But he adopted it only tentatively: it was just one possible form. In painting and sculpture he saw more definite possibilities, because they were historically freer. Neither of them had to face the problem which literature faced in entering upon a new stage. There were no such intrinsic changes wrought in colour and stone by decades of humanism as were wrought in language. All that sculpture and painting had to do was to escape from the works of humanism and revert to preferred barbaric modes, creating modern forms as if in primitive times—forms primitive, obedient to the conventions they accepted, therefore final, absolute, abstract. For poetry the problem was not so simple. It could not, it seemed, submit itself so facilely to an *as-if*: its expressive medium, language, had been intrinsically affected not only by the works in which it had been used but also by all the non-poetic uses of which language is capable.

This difference between poetry and the regular arts points to a variance in poetry and suggests the probable falsity of such philosophical generalizations on art as Hulme made. In his desire to coordinate and correctly generalize, he fell into the familiar philosophical confusion, the confusion of analogy. Art, for instance, is a philosophical term invented for the convenience of classification, not a term that poetry would naturally invent for itself, though painting and sculpture very well might for themselves. To the philosopher, however, the most accurate term is the most general rather than the most particular; and so to Hulme a common co-ordination of the "arts" seemed possible and necessary. Analogy is always false, but it is the strongest philosophical instrument of co-ordination. Since poetry as an art is not sufficiently regular, not sufficiently professional, it is to be made so by becoming more sculptural or more pictorial, by having grafted on it the values and methods of more professional arts.

While, then, by the use of analogy and other philosophical generalizations, a co-ordination and a simplification might be made in poetic theory and a satisfactory understanding of the poetic absolute and abstract poetic form reached, still language itself demanded purification; and this was a most complicated and difficult problem. It demanded first to be allowed to become disorganized until so loose grammatically that it could be reorganized as if afresh, without regard to how words and their combinations had been sympathetically affected by usage. It had to be as instrumentally pure as colour or stone. Words themselves would be reduced by this process to their least historical value. They would be cleansed of stale associations in order that they might be used primitively and abstractly. The purer they were the more eternally immediate and present they would be. In this way they could express the absolute at the same time as they were expressing the age.

Gertrude Stein's use of words may be looked on as such a purification. Her language is primitive and abstract. It is so primitive, indeed, that criticism has felt obliged to repudiate her work as a romantic vulgar barbarism, an expression of the personal crudeness of a mechanical age rather than a refined historical effort to restore a lost absolute to a group of co-ordinated creators. T. S. Eliot has said of Miss Stein's work that "it is not improving, it is not amusing, it is not interesting, it is not good for one's mind. But its rhythms have a peculiar hypnotic power not met with before. It has a kinship with the saxophone. If this is the future, then the future is, as it very likely is, of the barbarians. But this is the future in which we ought not to be interested."[8] Mr. Eliot was for the moment speaking from the civilized viewpoint: it seemed suddenly impossible to reconcile the crudities of any barbarism, however new, with the advanced historical state of the poetic mind and with the professional dignity of poetry which the new barbarism was invented to restore. A sincere attempt to do so was at once vulgar and obscure, like the work of Miss Stein. So except for such whole-hog literalness as hers modernist poetry has lacked the co-ordination to which modernist criticism subscribes; it has not had a controlling *ism* or school. This want would have been welcome if it had not meant an irreconcilability between criticism and workmanship which has made the latter a wasted performance.

Although Hulme has been Aristotelianized by the generation of modernist poets just passing, he arrived at art only through the failure of philosophy, and his theories of art must be derived from his criticism of philosophy. Philosophy had failed historically to keep "pure," to be "entirely objective and scientific." Philosophy was corrupted by the personal element. The personal element should have been carefully separated from the scientific element. The philosopher is the scientist of the absolute, but he unfortunately possesses an imperfect romancing human intelligence which confounds his study of the absolute with crude dreams and desires—the emotional, religious element. Philosophy can only be kept pure by cutting away the second element and making it an object of study, or rather of light philosophical curiosity. For it is this same intelligence or personalized humanity which in art upsets the absolute with caprice. The absolute is fixed; caprice is fictional. Recognize that the activities of the human intelligence are fictional, and fictional and relative become synonymous terms. How are we to determine what belongs to the absolute category, "the world of religious and ethical values," and what to the organic (the human, historical) category? By the principle of discontinuity. Decide that humanity is incapable of perfection, and perfection becomes dissociated from it, and the absolute is then absolute because it is discontinuous with organic humanity.

Now it might seem easier to enforce this distinction in philosophy than in art. But since all philosophy considers itself "pure" it is not likely to recognize the corrupting humanistic element when it appears; for this disguises itself in the same scientific language with which philosophy defines the absolute. Art, on the other hand, has grown more and more frankly humanistic and romantic—it rejoices in the fact that its values are fictional. Art, therefore, would not, like philosophy, resist the charge that it has allowed itself to be seduced by fictional values. It might even, if it were made to feel that its integrity was in danger, accept the formulas of a hypothetically pure philosophy in order to make its fiction substantial. It might tie itself to an absolute in order to make its fiction philosophically respectable. The fact that it owned to a fiction would merely mean that it lacked the arrogance natural to philosophy, which owns only to an absolute.

All this must have been felt by Hulme in his deprecation of the course philosophy had taken since the Renaissance and in his restatement of the absolute in terms of art rather than of philosophy. He did not, for instance, attack romanticism from the philosophical but from the literary point of view. The weaknesses of his generalizations are consequently more obvious than they would have been had his statement remained strictly philosophical. For philosophical statements are so general that they exclude illustrations and thus remain uncontrovertible until some one has the courage to challenge their consistency as generalizations, without resorting to illustrations. Furthermore, the literary statement never has the dogmatism of the philosophical statement: the philosopher speaks as for the Cosmic, the critic for a craft or himself or for those who may personally agree with him. Had Hulme been speaking as a philosopher he would not have attacked romanticism, he would have destroyed it, and he would have been unanswerable. It would have been impossible to point out that the idea of perfection dwelling in a non-human absolute is as romantic as the ideal of its dwelling in variable humanity; or that, since he could not admit perfection except in dissociation from humanity, he had merely invented the principle of discontinuity in order to invent from it the non-human absolute. By the way that philosophy defines itself it is protected from being revealed as a fiction. Hulme did not make a philosophy but a criticism of philosophy, and this was making a fiction. It is fiction to say, as this criticism does, that if the human intelligence recognizes an absolute and, of course, its own imperfection, and so shuts out from its fictional activities the "human plane," it must realize that its fiction will have a wholly "tragic significance" and will express the "futility of existence." It is romantic to say, while denouncing as romantic the meanings which the creative mind gives to its fictions, that these can only be valid if they confess their meaninglessness. Is not a belief in the lack of meaning in organic existence merely a new meaning that art is to adopt for the sake of the prestige given it by the metaphysics from which it is drawn?

Whether or not Hulme formally inaugurated the new barbarism in contemporary criticism is a fine and irrelevant point of history. Certainly a general degradation of the person was taking place in poetry at the time that he was writing—the first disorganized step toward professionalization and co-ordination. Poetry felt forced to objectify itself and to do this successfully it had to enter upon a philosophical career. Hulme's ardent neo-realism, or anti-humanism, supplied the doctrine necessary for this career. (His doctrine, a disappointment with philosophy, was itself in need of being legitimized and made positive by an application to practical aesthetics.) If poetry was to make its new career barbarically uniform, it had first of all to set about methodically exterminating the person. As there is nothing more absolute than the person and as there are therefore as many absolutes as distinct persons, the only way to get uniformity was to impose a single objective absolute, an abstract, regularly waved sea defeating eccentric individual configuration by the uninterrupted rhythm of its gross and monotonous detail.

The philosophical side of poetry's new career was simple. It defined the absolute, quoted the philosophers, dreamt of objectivity and spread its lap for the golden apples of art which it hoped would now drop out of its neo-realistic heaven. But no golden apples came, only glass marbles for criticism to play with while waiting for golden apples. The golden apples never came and criticism went on collecting more and more glass marbles. The reason why there have been no golden apples is that workmanship has not been able to take advantage of the serene privileges of the absolute. It has had to keep busy degrading the person and casting out from written and proposed verse all the romantic egotistical absolutes with which the tradition of poetry has ever been decorated. So literary criticism, as with Hulme, turns to admire other arts, such as painting, which are technically more capable of professional formality and period-uniformity.

The view that periods are or should be coherent time-lengths follows from a belief in an invariable, inferred absolute. Humanity itself is not absolute, but it has the privilege of dramatizing the absolute in time. If it could be physically as well as ethically or religiously (dramatically) uniform, it would have one single intact time-length. Personal time would be absent and require the same effort to be conceived as absolute time itself is by a physically variable humanity. It would, indeed, not affect the inherent absoluteness of time, it would merely make numerical repetitions of it. With a variable humanity, however, conforming to an ethically absolute time, personal time is a numerical variation, not a numerical repetition of it. And because absolute time can only be dramatically executed through personal time, it can be only relatively absolute: its absoluteness has to be inferred by comparison.

When humanity or a co-ordinated representative portion of humanity attempts to observe the absolute as strictly as possible in whatever form it is officially recognized at the time, and to compare its own relativeness with it continually, then we have a coherent time-length; we have classicism. When humanity falls in love with its own relativeness and ceases to compare its variability with an absolute, then we have romanticism. An unexaggerated romantic period is a collection of the remarkable and independent individuals who were alive in that period and of "forces" so distinctly varied that they are nearly recognizable as people—perhaps numerically representative of the less remarkable and independent individuals of the period. An exaggerated romantic period is one in which variation has assumed so great a significance that the period seems composed by one or two dominant personalities. The Napoleonic period was an exaggerated romantic period; so much so that every highly specialized personality seemed Napoleonic—the shadow of Napoleonism fell, in Europe, across the entire first half of the nineteenth century.

The antithesis of exaggerated romanticism is exaggerated classicism, which opposes impersonal to personal uniformity. Contemporary literary classicism is bent on enforcing a coherent time-length which shall rob personal variations of significance, and on connecting this time-length sympathetically with former classical periods, in order to make it as relatively absolute as possible. So it dismisses the Renaissance and joins itself directly to Mediaevalism; so it dismisses Darwinism as having given romantic significance to biological variation.

What impresses one most in tracing the new barbarism from its theoretical phase to its contact with actual creation is that here is a complicated machinery which, when set in motion and concentrated on what are its expressed ends, is capable of only the crudest mechanical gestures. Its subtleties become pomposities, its contributions to the cause that it has created, trivialities. Criticism has a great deal to say about criticism, which means that it is highly philosophical. But as it has very little that is relevant and helpful to say about poetry itself—not as a philosophical abstraction but as poems—criticism becomes, in practice, highly philosophical nonsense. Although it objects to the romantic disorganization in which there is not beauty but "beauties," it has no absolute canon of beauty to offer to the poetry which it is attempting to inspire but a primitive satire of beauties and a counsel to suppress the obvious because the obvious is often romantically (personally), therefore sentimentally beautiful. Although it insists that a fixed dogmatic beauty leaves the poet more free to achieve perfection, yet it has nothing better to offer than a few elementary suggestions and clues such as that "golden lad" is a beautiful classical phrase and "golden youth" a beautiful romantic phrase (Hulme). "The thing has got so bad now that a poem which is all dry and hard, a properly classical poem, would not be considered poetry at all. . . . They cannot see that accurate description is a legitimate object of verse."[9] Hulme did not stop just here, but however far he went (and this was not far) he could not get away from his battle with the past and help the present, although the present was his professed objective. Nor did he seem to realize the waste and absurdity of asking a forward-looking twentieth-century generation to arm itself against an early nineteenth-century bogey or against the Renaissance bogey itself.

We scarcely realize how crude a reference-word "classical" really is. If we consider its usage, even by an apparently careful writer like Hulme, we find it is nothing more than a term to apply to works designed with the intention that they shall become classics, and to those which have succeeded in this intention. If, moreover, we examine this intention, we discover that it is servilely concerned with technique and decency, but little with meaning, personal intensity or experimentation. Many of the difficulties of contemporary verse are indeed due to the attempt to reconcile the classical desideratum "dry and hard" with the necessity to experiment in order to fix beauty as criticism seems unable to fix it—experiment of course leading to romanticism. Romanticism, on the contrary, is not so concerned with technique or decency; it is more freakish, more ambitious, more amateurish. Because it is amateurish it is more serious: genuine amateurishness is a mixing of the making of a thing with the significance of its making. In exaggerated romanticism the significance of the making is more important than the problem of the making itself; it is the object of each individual exercise. In exaggerated classicism the professional sense is so dominant that the significance of the making is considered settled for the craft as a whole: there can be no making unless it is settled. Therefore in exaggerated romanticism we find an abnormal emphasis on perspective as in exaggerated classicism an abnormal absence of it. This abnormal absence of it, this forced naivety, is obedience to a discipline whose object is to prevent the use of form for speculation. The concentration of form on form means in classical terminology "abstract" or "pure" form. Speculation with form can also become, in romantic art, forced naivety—what Hulme wished to attack in Ruskinian seriousness.

The opposition is not, as Hulme cavalierly made it, of sophisticated levity to idiot-headed seriousness, or of fancy to imagination, but of a heavy, rigid, originally dull seriousness to a rather ingenuous, sometimes successful, often droll, though perhaps eventually dull seriousness. "Wonder must cease to be wonder," complained Hulme: but in the beginning, while there is wonder, there is always the chance of a surprise success in romanticism. In classicism, which sets out with a formal, defined intention, there is never the chance of success in this sense. If romantic freakishness generally quiets down to triteness and is for this reason dull, classical freakishness, of which there are so many contemporary specimens, is fixed and eternal from the outset and thus eternally dull. It cannot even be undermined by the influence it exercises because it is made with a kind of bigotry that immediately imposes itself rather than influences. A romantic movement must have an end, Hulme said, a discovery by a bigoted classicist full of significance: "movement" meaning the history and influence of romantic works, rather than the making of original romantic works themselves. A classicist, it is to be remarked, in attacking romanticism always attacks the end-products of a romantic movement, and the most feeble of these; as Hulme chooses to attack romanticism through Ruskinian seriousness rather than through the best of Keats, whom he admired; as he attacks humanism and the Renaissance at points where they break down. The conglomerativeness of romanticism makes it possible to attack it as a whole in this way through an assailable part, while the romanticist wishing to attack classicism must attack it as an integrated whole, with the result that it generally remains unattacked because the task seems too formidable.

Let me set down the most ingenuous expression of the romantic point of view that I can at the moment find. It is by William Kiddier, from a little book, one of a series, called "The Profanity of Paint."[10] First on colour, the medium of painting: "Colour is the soul of things! . . . I believe colour belongs to the fairies; it never comes quite within our grasp. It is borne upon the air, its chariot is the morning dew, and its paths the sunbeams. I have come to regard colour as a spiritual thing changing for ever, as all spiritual things do." Then on what we might call "The first principle": "Everything in the work should, in some special degree, contribute to the first idea. Nothing should be introduced for the sake of variety. . . . of a truth, trees can only be painted by the sympathetic hand, one that can make a simple group of all around him, selecting only those that, by their forms, shall contribute to the artistic sense *relation*. . . . Time counts for nothing. The trunk has been the work of centuries; and the season present brings forth the shoot; yea! a thousand years have gone between and both are in *relation*!" Now as this statement stands, we can say that it illustrates certain general characteristics of romanticism. The medium itself is related to a meaning, or spiritualized. Art is not the definite formation of form but human aspiration working through form, therefore tending to indefiniteness. *Relation* is apparently only an ambitious word for perspective. Contribution to a first idea is only romantic distortion of the elements of a picture to create a meaning. It does not imply in the artist a reverence for the absolute; for then his picture would have Meaning, but not a meaning in the human sense. If time counts for nothing to Mr. Kiddier, it is because he believes in continuity. It is eternal because human life to him is eternal, not because a discontinuity exists between "life" and the world of religious and ethical values which makes the time of the latter absolute, of the former relative.

Now let me set down the least ingenuous expression of the classical or barbaric point of view that I can at the moment find. It is by Ezra Pound, on the work of the sculptor Gaudier-Brzeska. Mr. Pound admires his work, we learn, because it is anti-Hellenic its chief formative influences were from archaic Greek, the Oceanic, the Egyptian, the Assyrian, the African, the Chinese—from strictly barbaric sources, in other words. He says, speaking of Gaudier's "The Dancer":

> This is almost a thesis of his ideas upon the use of pure form. We have the triangle and circle assented, *labled* almost, upon the face and right breast. Into these so-called "abstractions" life flows, the circle moves and elongates into the oval, it increases and takes volume in the sphere, or hemisphere of the breast. The triangle moves toward organism, it becomes a spherical triangle. . . . These two developed motifs work as themes in a fugue. We have the whole series of spherical triangles, as in the arm over the head, all combining and culminating in the great sweep of the back of the shoulders, as fine as any surface in all sculpture. The "abstract" or mathematical bareness of the triangle and circle are fully incarnate, made flesh, full of vitality and energy. The whole form series ends, passes into stasis with the circular base or platform.[11]

Mr. Pound quotes Gaudier-Brzeska himself: "Sculptural feeling is the appreciation of masses in relation. Sculptural ability is the defining of these masses by planes." Mr. Pound continues: "The sculptor must add to the power of imagining form-combination the physical energy required to cut this into the unyielding medium. He must have vividness of perception, he must have this untiringness, he must beyond that be able to retain his main idea unwaveringly during the time (weeks or months) of the carving." This statement may likewise be taken as a characteristic expression of classicism. We have an emphasis on the medium as material. The "main idea" is the proper and painstaking adjustment of the material to itself, its gradual assumption of definite form. The artist could not have the concentration necessary for this task, it is implied, if he did not exlude from it meaning in the human, relative sense. His work has an absolute quality, an "abstractness," to the degree to which he can exclude a meaning, to the degree to which his work exists in the world of religious and ethical value rather than in the world of biological striving. His forms would lack finality if they strove. There is no talk of spirituality, of everness, of sunbeams or of seasons bringing forth shoot. There is undoubtedly a fundamental first principle, but this is apparently so fundamental and so fixed that it is unnecessary and even forbidden to introduce it as the *subject* of a work. It is the point from which the artist begins rather than the one at which he aims.

Such seems to be the irreconcilability of these two statements as the expressions of two opposed ways of interpreting and applying the creative capacities. If, however, we examine them as two statements showing a difference of personal temperament in their authors, this hard and fast irreconcilability between romanticism and classicism disappears, and we see them both as somewhat arbitrary distinctions based on the temperamental variations likely to occur in people dealing with what is virtually the same process. Both temperaments may even be found to exist side by side in the same period. Mr. Kiddier is historically a modest contemporary of Mr. Pound's; and what, after all, does Mr. Kiddier say that Mr. Pound does not? He says that colour is the important thing in painting and that it is a very difficult and subtle medium. To say that it belongs to the fairies is only an extravagant and harmless way of saying that man has trouble in mastering it. To call colour a spiritual thing is merely an extravagant way of saying that, to use it properly, the artist must have high qualities, such as "insight, poignancy, retentiveness, plus the energy"—Mr. Pound's own list of the essentials in the "making of permanent sculpture." If Mr. Kiddier insists on a first idea, Mr. Pound insists on a main one. The artistic sense relation which for the former should show in the association of trees in a picture is, true enough, defined as a kind of emotional sympathy in the artist rather than as a necessary relationship between the "motifs" employed. But is this not merely a tenderer, more ingenuous version of Mr. Pound's own ingenuous enough remarks about the "complete thesis of principles" which the perfect statue apparently attains? Mr.

Kiddier, when he comes to Time, obviously lets his extravagance get control of him; there is a lack of respectability of a sort in this, unredeemed by any uniqueness of thought or expression. But it should not be overlooked, in Mr. Kiddier's defence, that it is part of his ingenuousness to pretend neither to respectability nor uniqueness; while Mr. Pound makes the uniqueness of his views respectable by quoting half a dozen barbarisms as his authorities, and his respectability unique by the use of a very limited language supposed to express literally the concrete problems of the artist. Romantic language such as Mr. Kiddier's soon becomes trite after the surprise of its first use wears off; language such as Mr. Pound uses (I do not wish, of course, to suggest that either Mr. Kiddier or Mr. Pound invented their language) soon becomes jargon, which means not only trite but senseless—for it is so limited that when it loses its literal sense its metaphorical sense (such as the application to poetry of terms invented for sculpture) becomes purely academic. We shall grow weary (if we have not already) of talk of circles, triangles, spheres, form, planes, stasis and masses sooner than talk of trees put in motion by the wind, fairies, sunbeams, seasons and the passing of centuries.

Shorn of its jargon, is there anything that Mr. Pound says which is not in Mr. Kiddier's philosophy? He says that the artist makes the mechanical exercises of his art breathe out life, that everything must be in *relation* (Mr. Kiddier's word), that the sculptor can make flesh out of stone as the colour-artist gets significant vibrations out of paint. His elaborate explanation of the technical merit of "The Dancer" is really a pedantic evasion of such words as "spirituality" about which Mr. Kiddier, if asked describe this statue, would in his ingenuousness not be squeamish. "The whole form-series ends, passes into statis with the circular base or platform" is merely the basic "sameness" or peacefulness of Mr. Kiddier's philosophy of art into which variety shall not be introduced for its own sake.[12] A romanticist would paraphrase Gaudier-Brzeska: "The sculptor must *feel* his subject as a whole and understand it minutely in its parts without allowing its soul to escape. More than this, he must be able to feel and understand with stone as well as with his heart and mind."[13] Whatever conviction this definition loses by its sentimentality, it gains by its applicability to more than one kind of sculpture—the romantic definition is always less strictly romantic than it would be if romanticism were a "movement" in the sense generally ascribed to it. That the language of classicism cannot be so easily applied to romantic works as that of romanticism to classical works would seem to show that it is classicism indeed which is always a movement doomed to have an end, and romanticism a vague name, sentimentally used on both sides, to describe the general human movement of art; if derogatively, to attack the vulgarity and incompetence in this movement.

The differences between the classical attitude and the romantic attitude, when considered as temperamental reactions to the same thing, seem to centre in the question of extravagance. The romanticist is not afraid of extravagance. He is so earnest that the danger of excess does not occur to him. The classicist is most of all afraid of extravagance. He has a self-conscious lack of confidence which prevents him from being earnest because he is aware of the danger of excess. This earnestness in the romanticist easily leads to vulgarity, this self-consciousness in the classicist, to snobbery. The reason why Hulme opposed fancy to the imagination was that he had a snobbish feeling against the imagination from its being associated with many vulgarities, not from any real objection to imagination itself: for fancy to him was merely an improved, more technical, narrower imagination. "Abstract" is another "classical" word that has come to have a thoroughly snobbish connotation. It generally means: lacking in sentimental allusions to fairies, trees, spirituality, time, spring. Likewise "mathematical" and "geometric" prove themselves to mean lacking in vulgar humanity, having non-vital realism. The classical artist is a snob against himself. He therefore separates his art from his nature and thus art from nature. This is the history of discontinuity and the abstraction of art. Art, in Hulme's words, is created to satisfy a desire. The desire appears to be, in theory, the desire for art itself; to create a discontinuity in man by isolating art from nature. So art is not the creation of a fiction, but a very gloomy feeling in man about his own nature. Why this is not a romantic attitude—for the romantic includes some very gloomy feelings, indeed, about the nature of man—is that the romantic gloomy feelings do not seem to be gloomy or pessimistic enough. Romantic gloom, of course, can be extravagantly depressing or hysterical. But gloom for the classicist is not final, abstract or mathematical unless it is just gloom, without being either depressing or hysterical. Absolute gloom is so gloomy that it does not have to be gloomy: if gloom is gloomy it becomes vulgarized. Classical art is therefore created to satisfy a desire for gloom which is really, however, a snobbish feeling about romantic gloom.

IV

It has been seen that contemporary criticism, the philosophical portion of contemporary poetic activity, has attempted to bring about some order in the views commonly held about poetry. By doing this it has hoped to bring about an order in the actual writing of poetry. The only order there has been in poetry for the last hundred and thirty-five years has been a superficial uniformity due to a confused sympathy of sentiment and imagery in the language in which it was written. But there has been no fundamental professional sense of the eighteenth-century sort. The mental background has been anarchic and amateurish. When contemporary criticism expresses its respect for the eighteenth century it is, of course, praising its professional sense. It is impossible to believe that it is praising eighteenth-century poetry as such, in which the sentiment of professional uniformity lacked the energy that might have been supplied to it by anarchy and amateurishness.

The problem of the present-day poet, therefore, who feels himself responsible to the problem raised by criticism, is a very difficult one. He must react against the unprofessional and superficial uniformity which romanticism brought about—he must maintain a professional independence of sentiment and imagery—and at the same time avoid anarchy and amateurishness. He must resign from the emotional brotherhood which poetry formed from a loose romantic social sense and attach himself to the organized metaphysics of poetry professionalized in the narrowest possible social sense as an art-and-craft.

We may say that the problem will be to a large extent solved by the poet's originality and the discipline that should go with it if it is to be effective originality. And it is true that the successes in contemporary poetry have been those which have been able to combine originality and discipline. But in general the burden of responsibility has been with originality; discipline has been distorted, teased and distracted by the lack, in criticism, of immediate suggestiveness, a failure which is aggravated by the dogmatic character of its theorizing. Criticism assumes all the prerogatives which belong to creation without assuming any of its concrete responsibilities. It limits its share in these responsibilities to a negative and irresponsible taste and envelops itself in a forbidding cloud of snobbery.

Criticism says: "Art refers to an absolute. It must recognize a first principle. Every work must imply this first principle." "What," is the creative question, "is the first principle? A work cannot imply it by interrogation; that would be romantic." But the first principle is not stated. It seems part of the consistency of the system that it shall not be stated. It must be derived from the system in such a way that its finality shall not be impaired by its relation to contemporary history. The age itself must invent a provisional first principle, the corporeal representative of the absolute. The absolute cannot be absolute and appear in person. Art is ideal action. It does not so much create "things" as reveal "things" with the things it creates. Its purpose is "to pierce through the veil placed between us and reality" (Hulme) with the work, not to lodge reality in the work itself.[14] The work is a kind of beautiful behaviour, but the beauty of this behaviour must not be made to inhere in the work, for this would mean a confusion of standards. Beauty must be inferred, its sameness verified. Variety is in the instrumentality of art, not in its meaning. Its meaning is so *same* that it can only be "expressed," it cannot be immediately present. The belief in the possibility of its being immediately present is a perverted romantic notion.

Thus the absolute, beauty, the first principle, remain persistently elusive unless supplied by the "age." The critical energy of the poet is supposed to be more concretely responsible than the creative energy of criticism: half the energy of the poet, if not more, is to be consumed in making the age yield its version of the first principle. This version is known as a "theme." If the theme is absent it is through the combined fault of the poet and the age. The poet should have the power of identifying himself with the temporal extent of his age, of realizing his proper theme; and the age should lend itself to this identification. If this happy union is not effected, criticism takes the attitude that it is very significant that it has not been effected, that it is indeed too bad and that the poet will have to do the next best thing, that is, write about this very significant and deplorable handicap. "The dissociation" (of vision and subject), says Allen Tate in his Foreword to a volume of poems by Hart Crane, "appears decisively for the first time in Baudelaire."[15] Theme-ishness, Mr. Tate wishes to suggest, wore itself out. This is not to be interpreted as a reflection on the theme-ishness of the absolute, but apparently on history, which has not been able to sustain the succession of themes, and on poets, who have, because of history, been forced to desert this succession. Nor does it contradict the unexpressed first principle or the theoretical necessity for a theme. "For while Mr. Eliot might have written a more ambitiously unified poem," Mr. Tate further says, "the unity would have been false; tradition as unity is not contemporary." Tradition, he means, is unity, and contemporary criticism is busy saying this; but contemporary poetry is not unity because it is busy proving how distressing the absence of unity is and also paying the penalty for the sins of romanticism, which disregarded tradition as unity and so in its anarchic enthusiasm developed no unity but a feeble universalization of poetic language. "For," he goes on to say in a few sentences, "the comprehensiveness and lucidity of any poetry, the capacity for poetry being assumed as proved, are in direct proportion to the availability of a comprehensive and perfectly articulated given theme." This theme being temporarily absent (Mr. Tate does not say who should have articulated the theme. Not the poet, since the theme is given? Nor history, since this would imply a critical function which Mr. Tate would surely not admit in history?

The only deduction possible is that criticism, for no discoverable reason, has decided to be coy), "the important contemporary poet has the rapidly diminishing privilege of reorganizing the subjects of the past," Mr. Tate concludes.

T. S. Eliot composed such a résumé in *The Waste Land*. James Joyce attempted the same sort of thing in a more destructive way in his long progressive use of period literary styles in *Ulysses*. Gertrude Stein, lacking the sophistication of either of these, refused to be baffled by criticism's haughty coyness and, taking the absolute and beauty and the first principle quite literally, saw no reason, all these things being so, why we should not have a theme, why indeed we cannot assume "a perfectly articulated given theme." If everybody assumed this perfectly articulated given theme (and no one has yet shown satisfactorily why, fortified by such a criticism, we should not), everybody would understand Gertrude Stein. By combining the functions of critic and poet and taking everything around her very literally and many things for granted which others have not been naive enough to take so, she has done what every one else has been ashamed to do. No one but Miss Stein has been willing to be as ordinary as simple, as primitive, as stupid, as barbaric as successful barbarism demands.

Does no one but Miss Stein realize that to be abstract, mathematical, thematic, anti-Hellenic, anti-Renaissancist, anti-romantic, we must be barbaric? What has happened? We have had enough triangles, circles, spheres and hemispheres to satisfy any barbaric geometric craving, and yet it is certain that triangles, circles, spheres, and hemispheres have passed: the London *Times* recently criticized a young artist's work which was of a geometric type as "old-fashioned." If the geometric type (which Hulme opposed to the vital type) has passed (as it has) it must be because it was romantic (a romantic movement must have an end) and because it was surprised and defeated by its own romanticism.

We have seen how near the surface romanticism lurked in Mr. Pound's philosophy. We discover Hulme's absolute, too, to have been a pessimist's deification of pessimism, a sentimental abstraction of despair. Hulme's romanticism is finally and completely confessed in his attachment to Bergson. Bergson's attraction is that in rescuing the fundamentally romantic idea of evolution from its idealization, evolutionary progress, he invented an elaborate, pleasurable and dreamy way for the modern classicist to be barbaric. By interpreting evolution as an intensive instead of an extensive process he kept the movement and variations of evolution but eliminated the objectionable enlargement of significance with which humanity generally accompanies its movement and variations. By calling the true intelligence of this process intuitive rather than intellectual he discredited the civilized personality of the human mind: he made intelligence a principle instead of a faculty. By defining the time-world as an absolute duration which continuously interpenetrated itself and thus continuously produced new forms, he suggested a movement in the absolute without attacking its absoluteness; he made romanticism seem classical, and, above all, kept an important place for originality in this system without displacing discipline.

The devotion of the modern classicist to originality is the most serious flaw in his metaphysical technique. As a result of his romantic weakness for it, discipline is perverted. Yet he cannot abandon originality, however it perverts discipline, because he despises and wishes to suppress the vulgar undisciplined originality of ordinary humanity. So his classicism is designed to represent ordinary humanity only theoretically, which means that it really represents those who have extraordinary power or superiority over ordinary humanity. This flaw was very obvious in Hulme's idea of the nature of the artist's vision. To Hulme, the artist saw something that no one else saw, he directly communicated "individuality and the freshness of things": the only suggestion of classicism in this being the peculiar emphasis on "things."[16] Speaking again of the artist, he said: "It is because he realizes the inadequacy of the usual that he is obliged to invent." Direct communication, it is further implied, is hindered by the long romantic history of society: democratic communism of speech has destroyed the priesthood of the artist to the absolute. The modern classicist, to believe in the absolute, must believe in communism, but in autocratic communism: communism permitting of originality in the autocrat. The representative authority of the artist comes, it appears, from his superiority: he is the autocrat of originality.

A discrepancy multiplies. How is originality to remain consistent with the classicism of the new barbarism when every increase in originality seems, as in modernist poetry, a movement in the direction of romanticism, a widening of the breach between criticism and workmanship? "The artist must discover," criticism would reply, "classical originality: he must invent an original type." For a time it seemed as if the geometric type was the sought-for original type. But it failed as an experiment in original classicism because it was only a sophisticated imitation, or rather caricature, of perhaps the most ordinary type of art in the past. And it is hard to see, indeed, how the pursuit of an original type can get any farther than a caricature of the ordinary. The possibilities might seem greater in literature, where it has been permissible for human personality to contribute to this desired combination of originality and conventionality. But here, too, the creative limit seems to be reached in caricature; in Joyce's Leopold Blum and in Eliot's Prufrock and other "low types," originality proves to be, after all, only an attack on a degenerated ordinary. *Ordinary* and *original* therefore cannot be used by classicism as reconcilable terms; or rather their use as such reveals the contradiction in their use.

The "direct communication" by which originality is to be transmitted contains a further contradiction. Directness of communication means immediate ideal intelligibility. But since language has been degraded by its experiences, much of the originality will have to be employed in attacking the ordinary language of communication: direct communication, like the original type, will be able to go no farther than an obscure caricature of ordinary language, as in the dialogue in Mr. Eliot's *Fragment of a Prologue*.[17] And caricature is indirect, erratic, romantic. The poetry of Edith Sitwell is but one instance in contemporary poetry of the romantic caricature of language which contemporary classicism has fostered. Another aspect of the same general flaw is the incompatibility of the "things" which are supposed to be revealed in the direct communication ("things" in which apparently the first principle inheres) with the talent of the artist to see things "as no one else sees them." The barbaric absolute, the divine source of "things," wherever it has prevailed naturally, has always been marked by a penetrating obviousness. The Pyramids are penetratingly obvious: they nearly make absoluteness synonymous with obviousness.

Creative originality can only be consistent with barbaric communism if it is not *superior* creative originality. The only kind of originality which can see "things" "as no one else sees them" for barbaric mass-humanity, for human ordinariness, is mass-originality: some mystical, large-scale process in which the artist is chosen as a seeing instrument without his ordinariness being destroyed. He may be regarded by his tribe as divinely inspired to communicate directly, but inspired in ordinariness. The ideal barbaric artist is superior in ordinariness rather than in originality. For a long time the new barbarism has been wasting itself on disguised romantics while Gertrude Stein quietly has gone on practising a coherent barbarism under its very nose without encouragement or recognition. Her only crime has been that she has followed directions and disciplined away discrepancies. She has been able to do this because she is completely without originality. Everybody is unable to understand her and thinks that this is because she is too original or is trying too hard to be original. But she is only divinely inspired in ordinariness. She uses language automatically to record pure, ultimate obviousness. She makes it capable of direct communication not by caricaturing language in its present stage-attacking decadence with decadence—but by purging it of its discredited experiences. None of the words Miss Stein uses have ever had any experience. They are no older than her use of them, and she is herself no older than her age conceived barbarically.

> Put it there in there there where they have it
> Put it there in there there and they halve it
> Put it there in there there and they have it
> Put it there in there there and they halve it[18]

None of these words, it can be seen, has ever had any history before this. The design that Miss Stein makes of them is literally abstract and mathematical because they are etymologically transparent and commonplace, mechanical but not eccentric. If they possess originality it is the originality of gross automatism. Their author is a large-scale mystic, she is the darling priest of cultured infantilism to her age—if her age but knew it.

> Nothing changes from generation to generation except the thing seen, and that makes a composition.[19]

Her admission that there are generations does not contradict her belief in an unvarying first principle. Times does not vary, only the sense of time.

> Automatically with the acceptance of the time-sense comes the recognition of the beauty and once the beauty is accepted the beauty never fails anyone.[20]

Beauty has no history, time has no history; only the time-sense has history. When the time-sense acclaims a beauty which was not at first recognized, the finality of this beauty is at once established, it is as though it had never been denied. All beauty is equally final. The reason why the time-sense if realized reveals the finality or classicalness of beauty is that it is the feeling of beginning, of primitiveness and freshness which is each age's or generation's version of time.

> Beginning again and again and again explaining composition and time is a natural thing.
>
> It is understood by this time that everything is the same except composition and time, composition and the time of the composition and the time in the composition.[21]

Originality of vision, then, is invented not by the artist but by the collective time-sense. The artist does not see "things" "as no one else sees them." He sees those objective "things" in which the absolute is repeatedly verified, personalized and represented by the age. He sees concretely and expressively what every one else who is possessed of the time-sense has an unexpressed intuition of: the time-sense may not be generally and particularly universal; but this does not make the artist's vision, even his originality of vision, less collective or less universal.

> The composition is the thing seen by every one living in the living they are doing, they are the composing of the composition that at the time they are living is the composition of the time in which they are living. It is that that makes living a thing they are doing. Nothing else is different, of that almost any one can be certain. The time when and the time of and the time in that composition is the natural phenomena of that composition and of that perhaps every one can be certain.[22]

All this Gertrude Stein has understood and executed logically because of the perfect simplicity of her mind. Believing implicitly in an absolute, she has not been bothered to doubt the bodily presence of a first principle in her own time. Since she is alive and everybody around her seems to be alive, why of course there is an acting first principle, there is composition. This acting first principle provides a "perfectly articulated given theme" because there is time, and everybody, and the beginning again and again and again, and composition. In her primitive good-humour she does not find it necessary to trouble to define the theme. The theme is to be inferred from the composition. The composition is clear because the language means nothing but what it means in her using of it. The composition is final because it is "a more and more continuous present including more and more using of everything and continuing more and more beginning and beginning and beginning."[23] She creates this atmosphere of continuousness principally by her progressive use of the tenses of verbs, by an intense and unflagging repetitiousness and by an artificially assumed and regulated child-mentality: the child's time-sense is so vivid that an occurrence is always consecutive to itself, it goes on and on, it has been going on and on, it will be going on and on; a child does perhaps feel the passage of time, does to a certain extent feel itself older than it was yesterday because yesterday was already to-morrow even while it was being yesterday.

> Alfred as I was saying was in Gossols when he was a very young one and when he was a little older than a young one. Sometimes then later he saw a little sometimes of Olga the sister of the first governess the Herslands had had in their Gossols living staying with them. Some-

> times the Wyman fairily made up to him. This is the way he had all these in him this that I am now beginning describing. This is now beginning to be a history of him, a history of Alfred Hersland of all the being and all the living in him.[24]

This is how Gertrude Stein wrote in 1906 and this is how she was still writing in 1926. Writing by always beginning again and again and again keeps everything different and everything the same. It creates duration but makes it absolute by preventing anything from happening in the duration.

> And after that what changes what changes after that, after that what changes and what changes after that and after that and what changes and after that and what changes after that.[25]

The composition has a theme because it has no theme. The words are a self-pursuing, tail-swallowing series and are therefore thoroughly abstract. They achieve what Hulme called, but could not properly envisage, a "perpendicular," an escape from the human horizontal plane.[26] They contain no references, no meanings, no caricatures, no jokes, no despairs. They are so automatic that it is even inexact to speak of Miss Stein as their author: they create one another. The only possible explanation of lines like the following is that one word or combination of words creates the next.

> As long as head as short as said as short as said as long as head.[27]
>
> . . . . .
>
> A little away
> And a little away.
> Everything away.
> Everything and away.
> Everything and away.
> Away everything away.[28]

This is repetition and continuousness and beginning again and again and again.

Nothing that has been said here should be understood as disrespectful to Gertrude Stein. What has been said has been said in praise and not in contempt. She has courage, clarity, sincerity, simplicity. She has created a human mean in language, a mathematical equation of ordinariness, which leaves one with a tender respect for that changing and unchanging slowness that is humanity and Gertrude Stein. Humanity—one learns this from Gertrude Stein but not from contemporary poetry—is fundamentally a nice person; and so is Gertrude Stein.

Having, in her recent essay *Composition As Explanation*, explained composition and composed explanation and made language serve critical and creative aims at the same time, she then proceeds to speak of romanticism as no other contemporary critic with a classical bias has been able to do; she speaks of it as a role which composition may play when it is being the same thing that it is when it plays the rôle of classicism.

> Everything is the same except composition and as the composition is different and always going to be different everything is not the same.[29]

We may draw from this a definition of classicism: it is the sameness of the differentness of composition. The definition of romanticism means only a shift of emphasis, and Miss Stein does this for us.

> Romanticism is then when everything being alike everything is naturally simply different, and romanticism.[30]

Romanticism is the differentness of the sameness of composition.

> After all this, there is that, there has been that that there is a composition and that nothing changes except composition the composition and the time of and the time in the composition.[31]

The time in the composition is its sameness and its differentness, its classicism and its romanticism. If the composition is to have lastingness it must return to the sameness. If the composition is to have life it must begin again and again and again with the differentness. Such seems to be Miss Stein's philosophy of history in art. But as the composition is something which goes on and on in a continuous present and using of everything and beginning again and again and again, it does not seem to matter which comes first, romanticism or classicism, or whether a work or attitude is attributed to one or to the other or whether, indeed, it is ever necessary to refer to either.

Both, however, have a certain strategical usefulness. Classicism is a historical formula invented by criticism for any period of history whose art can be looked on as a whole. It is very strictly a term for the past and for the past only. However good a work may seem, it cannot be properly called classical unless it can be associated with other things called classical. The word classical carries with it the weight of all works that have ever been called classical. The impressiveness of a "classic" is in the implication that it belongs in the company of other great works and, regardless of its time, really dates from long ago, from the time when the past was so solid that everything was classical. Everything up to a certain point in history, the Renaissance say, was classical, even the Hellenic, which has really only lost respectability because of its Renaissance and post-Renaissance influence. This is the ironical force of "a modern classic." Classicism is what Miss Stein means by "distribution and equilibration."

But when "distribution and equilibration" is urged or attempted while the composition is in process, when criticism recommends a contemporaneous classicism, then it is really being the criticism of the future, looking back on its own period (since classicism can only refer to the past) and attempting to order its own period backwards. This is why a division between modernist composition and modernist criticism is inevitable. The criticism is talking backwards. The composition, because its time is a continuous present, is talking forwards. Criticism drops a perpendicular at the point where the continuous horizontal of composition begins again with the contemporary time-sense. The point where the perpendicular meets the horizontal is unreal in the perpendicular, because past and therefore refuted by the presentness of the point on the horizontal.

Romanticism has a broader usefulness. Referring to differentness rather than sameness, it is a word for the present rather than for the past: the farther works are in the past the more same they seem, the nearer to the present, the more different. Romanticism is more useful if only by the greater of number of works to which it may refer, also because it characterizes without definitely classifying—"romanticism, which was not a confusion but an extrication" as Gertrude Stein says. Afterwards comes the distribution and equilibration, "there must be time that is distributed and equilibrated." Thus every period afterwards is in a way classical. But, while the composition is going on, it is not same, it is different, it is "an extrication." Contemporary composition which may be in sympathy with the classicism of contemporary criticism must nevertheless in practice react against it; composition cannot go on if it tries to be self-consciously same. It must be different if only because it must have different authors. Gertrude Stein, an ideal "same" author for a classical period, is nevertheless many different authors in one. She might seem more intelligible if it were possible to read her as many authors.

3
The Facts in the Case of Monsieur Poe

Poe stock goes up and up; and what with Close-up's and Appreciations and Gups, Tips, Hints, Revelations, Communications, Studies, Essays, Beauties, Congratulations, Intimations, Discoveries, Embroideries, Theories, Comparisons, Editions, Diapasons, literary criticism has now another yard of rope with which to hang itself. Poe has come to be, at first slowly, then with increasing rapidity, one of the "good names." He may be evoked by advanced criticism when references run down; there is an alliance of reciprocal favours between Poe and advanced criticism. There is an alliance between Poe and less advanced criticism because he has passed the required exhumation period and may be personally reclaimed through those poems and tales by which he has always been dear to the hearts of parlour reciters and editors of short-story classics. He has been found to rhyme with Rimbaud. He has been found to yield a thesis subject. He has added to the vocabulary and the voraciousness of amateur psychologists of the abnormal. He is an example of persecuted genius, wayward genius, practical genius, supreme artifice in art, supreme art in artifice, narcotics, metaphysics, dream-life, love-life, and fate. Much of the stimulus for this enthusiasm has been furnished by the publication of hitherto unaccessible documents. Contemporary criticism, however, is very little interested in correcting and stabilizing the Poe legend. The popularity of Poe is due rather to his usefulness to criticism than to criticism's usefulness to him. There is an arrogance, a restlessness, a high pitch in the name which gives an air of irrefutability to critical jargon. Nor does literal investigation, when it occurs, yield anything more than the theory of the investigator, since the subject, being cloudy but shallow, does not complicate its usefulness as a laboratory specimen by unsuspected depth or richness.[1]

For Poe was too much of a mystery-man to himself to remain a mystery-man to others. His life, like his poems, had an immediate journalistic communicability, a mean public confidentialness. It gives little cause for speculation on motives, misconstructions, secrecies—Poe is a biographical failure if for no other reason than that he is too obvious. A Poe cult can have no science, it can have only sentiment, and is therefore completely humourless, as humourless indeed as Poe was himself. A few trivial instances of this sentiment from "a monograph now in preparation" and printed in one of the many Poe articles to be found in the index of any current American (or English or French) periodical will perhaps suggest the extent to which the cheap-jack figure of Poe has hypnotized the good sense of contemporary letters. "Poe later became estranged from Hirst when that worthy parodied two lines of 'The Haunted Palace' thus:

> Never nigger shook a shin-bone
> In a dance-house half so fair.

Poe was particularly sensitive to such breaches of good taste." The lines parodied will be found to read:

> Never seraph spread a pinion
> Over fabric half so fair![2]

It is easy to understand that Poe was sensitive in the matter of parody; but it seems impossible that the worst good taste could have resisted the invitation to parody in these foolish lines. Again, the same writer excuses Poe's irascible nerves on the ground that "poor Poe," as "a reviewer of current books, could not escape reading what came from the press, and the literary output of that day was in most instances unconscionably trashy." Very true. But it did not occur to the author of this article that some of this unconscionable trash was contributed by the pen of Edgar Allan Poe. If "Poe must have gasped at such figures as:

> My love, good night! let slumber steep
> In poppy juice those melting eyes . . .

may we not be permitted to gasp at such figures as:

> The very roses' odours
> Died in the arms of the adoring airs.[3]

"Strangely enough," says the same writer, "it is quite impossible to determine whether it was friendship or fear which held Poe in restraint whenever he noticed publicly the occasional writings of Mr. English." He defends Poe by advancing the theory that Poe wrote "tongue in cheek, keeping, however, always within a safe limit, so as not openly to offend one who seems to have had some strange control over him." Poe himself says that he always wrote of English in "the most unmistakable irony." But if it is recalled that Poe over and over again found beauties in verse not better than English's, and often worse—especially in the work of contemporary poetesses, likewise that Poe had at his command only the bluntest, heaviest kind of *sarcasm*, it will be seen that Poe was neither behaving strangely nor "writing tongue in cheek"—a performance of which Poe was constitutionally incapable. He was merely exercising his usual critical policy, a form of lively, self-protective opportunism. Most of the illustrations in Poe's critical writings are from the works of fellow-editors and fellow-journalists, most of them absurd, as absurd as the verse of that absurd period so consistently was—including Poe's. A real perspective of Poe's "verse" can be had only by considering it in relation to its contemporaneous fellow-verse, in emulation of which it was written—the verse, say, of Neal, Pinkney, Willis, Longfellow. It was not better, it was only more flashy. By his vulgar capacity for measuring the limits of "popular taste" (his favourite slogan) he soon outclassed Longfellow, a more genuine if more tame talent specializing in the same effects as himself. Contrary to the impression given by Poe's numerous defenders, his reputation has never been neglected. Poe never neglected it himself during his lifetime. With the mystery tales, which naturally reached "popular taste" sooner, as a background, and the melancholy autobiographical tone of the name as a literary headline, it has never been neglected since.

Looking over the history of his reputation to the opening of the twentieth century, we find him favourably and fully represented in the major anthologies published during that time: for example, in Griswold's *Poets and Poetry of America* published during his lifetime; in Dana's *Household Book of Poetry*, published eight years after his death; in Bryant's *Library of Poetry and Song*, published in 1870; and in Stedman's 1900 *American Anthology* in which the editor says, "He gave a saving grace of melody and illusion to French classicism, to English didactics, to the romance of Europe from Italy to Scandinavia." He was a schoolroom classic long before he became one of the watchwords of advanced criticism; and the romantic ill-fame of his personal life, wholly out of proportion to the facts, which read neither wickedly nor impressively, increased, if anything, the legend which Poe himself seems to have invented.

The typical publisher's notice of a new Poe volume generally reads as follows:

A Publication of Startling Content
EDGAR ALLAN POE—THE MAN
With a Foreword by . . . known as the "greatest living authority on Poe"
NOW THE TRUTH IS KNOWN

Since Poe's death, seventy-seven years ago, a sympathetic following has had to accept statements of Poe's indulgences. This monumental work is a defence, substantiated by conclusive evidence, of the character of America's greatest literary genius.

More than Sixty-Five Per Cent. New Material, letters, records, documents and illustrations are here published for the first time. Poe, the man of mystery, is revealed in a standard, final biography, the only complete, illustrated life of him "whose imperishable fame is in all lands."

Two Volumes. 1,649 Pages. 500 Illustrations.

Even more than as "America's greatest literary genius" Poe stands as a symbol of "the American grain" (to use a phrase of Dr. William Carlos Williams') to those to whom Americanism means not precisely patriotism, but a certain dashing intellectual concept.[4] Mr. H. L. Mencken, for example, who, like Dr. Williams, is an exemplar of Americanism in the large and luxurious sense, is not exactly patriotic; but a worshipper of Poe. Poe to Dr. Williams is not, as he must be to some extent to Mr. Mencken and as he was to the Reverend Rufus Wilmot Griswold, the descendant, however wayward, of a respectable Baltimore family; he is "a new De Soto," an American pioneer clearing away old-world clutter by "the plainness of his reasoning upon elementary grammatical, syntactical and prosodic grounds."[5] Some of the old-world clutter Poe thought worthy of preserving from destruction and immortalizing along with new-world clutter that he did not have the courage to clear away (the poetry of Mr. Cranch, Mrs. Welby, Mr. Pinkney, etc.) was the poetry of Lord Byron, Thomas Moore, Alfred Tennyson, Thomas Hood, etc. He even patronized Longfellow, Bryant and Lowell until he began to feel that he was being snubbed by them. Then Longfellow became Professor Longfellow and Mr. L. is challenged to a sparring match. It is difficult not to sympathize with Lowell, who wrote:

Here comes Poe with his Raven, like Barnaby Rudge
Three fifths of him genius, and two fifth sheer fudge;
Who talks like a book of iambs and pentameters;

In a way to make all men of common sense damn meters;
Who has written some things for the best of their kind;
But somehow the heart seems squeezed out by the mind.[6]

Indeed, Mr. L. has shown himself, if anything, too tolerant.

Three-fifths of him sheer fudge and two-fifths sheer fudge would have been more accurate. But Mr. L. was a contemporary and a gentleman.

Another element of Poe's "originality," according to Dr. Williams, is his "native vigour," his rejection of "colonial imitation." Poe said, on this subject: "Because it suited us to construct an engine in the first instance, it has been denied that we could compose an epic in the second. . . . But this is purest insanity." And again "We have snapped asunder the leading-strings of our British Grandmama, and, better still, we have survived the first hours of our novel freedom, the first licentious hours of hobbledehoy braggadocio and swagger." The only hobbledehoy braggadocio and swagger to be found in early nineteenth-century American literature is in Poe; and then it is not anti-British, but anti-Mr. Lowell, anti-Professor Longfellow, anti-Mr. English or anti-anyone who could be construed in any sense as anti-Poe. Dr. Williams, moreover, is not apparently aware that literary independence was the favourite polite topic of the American Victorian essayist. Even the objectionable Mr. Lowell, in his essay *On a Certain Condescension in Foreigners*, wrote:

> But whatever we might do or leave undone, we were not genteel, and it was uncomfortable to be continually reminded that, though we should boast that we were the great West till we were black in the face, it did not bring us an inch nearer to the world's West-End. That sacred enclosure of respectability was tabooed to us. The Holy Alliance did not inscribe us on its visiting list. The Old World of wigs and orders and liveries would shop with us, but we must ring at the area-bell and not venture to awaken the more august clamors of the knocker. Our manners, it must be granted, had none of those graces that stamp the caste of Vere de Vere, in whatever museum of British antiquities they may be hidden. In short, we were vulgar.[7]

Dr. Williams might be enlightened by similar passages in Emerson and other Victorians. "Lowell and Bryant," continues Dr. Williams, "were concerned with literature, Poe with the soul." This of the Poe whose energy was consumed before its due time in journalistic pettifoggery, what Dr. Williams calls Poe's "slaughter of banality." Poe's banal slaughter of banality. Dr. Williams reaches the climax of his enthusiasm in finding in him a foreshadowing of Gertrude Stein: "Sometimes he used words so playfully his sentences seem to fly away from sense."

> Now Doubt—now Pain
> Come never again,
> For her soul gives me sigh for sigh,
> And all day long
> Shines, bright and strong,
> Astarte within the sky,
> While ever to her dear Eulalie upturns her matron eye—
> While ever to her young Eulalie upturns her violet eye.[8]

No, this is Poe, not Miss Stein. But Dr. Williams is perhaps referring to Poe's prose?

> It was in no placid temper, I say, that the metaphysician drew up his chair to its customary station by the hearth. Many circumstances of a perplexing nature had occurred during the day to disturb the serenity of his meditations. In attempting *des œeufs à la Princesse*, he had unfortunately perpetrated an *omelette à la Reine*; the discovery of a principle of ethics had been frustrated by the overturning of a stew; and last, not least, he had been thwarted in one of those admirable bargains which he at all times took such special delight in bringing to a successful termination. But in the chafing of his mind at these unaccountable vicissitudes, there did not fail to be mingled some degree of that nervous anxiety which the fury of a boisterous night is so well calculated to produce. Whistling to his more immediate vicinity the large water-dog we have spoken of before, and settling himself uneasily in his chair, he could not help casting a wary and unquiet eye toward those distant recesses of the apartment whose inexorable shadows not even the red fire-light itself could more than partially succeed in overcoming. Having completed a scrutiny whose exact purpose was perhaps unintelligible to himself, he drew close to his seat a small table covered with books and papers, and soon became absorbed in the task of retouching a voluminous manuscript, intended for publication on the morrow.[9]

Or

> And it is the greater number of spondees in the Greek than in the English—in the ancient than in the modern tongue—which has caused

> it to fall out that while these eminent scholars were groping for a Greek hexameter, which is a spondaic rhythm varied now and then by dactyls, they merely stumbled, to the lasting scandal of scholarship, over something which, on account of its long-leggedness, we may as well term a Feltonian hexameter, and which is a dactylic rhythm, interrupted, rarely, by artificial spondees which are no spondees at all, and which are curiously thrown in by the heels at all kinds of improper and impertinent points.[10]

—Such is the language (to disregard the inaccuracy of the content of the second quotation) which, to Dr. Williams (and others), seems "to fall back continuously to a bare surface exhausted by having reached no perch in tradition."[11]—"Seldom a long or sensuous sentence. . . . Thought, thought, mass . . ."—"There is nothing offensively 'learned' there, nothing contemptuous, even in the witty tricks with bogus Latin which he plays on his illiterate public, which by *its* power, in turn, *permits* him an originality, *allows* him, even when he is satiric, an authenticity—since he is not seeking to destroy but to assert, candidly, and to defend *his own*."—"His greatness is in that he turned his back and faced inland, to originality, with the identical gesture of a Boone."—"And for *that* reason he is unrecognized." For what reason, and by whom? By his illiterate public, and because he tried to palm off bogus Latin on them?

Poe stayed against the thin edge, driven to be heard by the battering racket about him to a distant screaming—the pure essence of his locality.

The best poem is *To One in Paradise.*

A few lines of this poem should be reproduced:

> For, alas! alas! with me
>   The light of Life is o'er!
>   "No more—no more—no more—"
>   (Such language holds the solemn sea
>   To the sands upon the shore)
>   Shall bloom the thunder-blasted tree
>   Or the stricken eagle soar![12]

An inhibition composed of uneven parts of snobbism and loyalty generally inspires modern Poe enthusiasts to quote Poe in his less famous achievements. In Dr. Williams it is three parts loyalty to prefer *To One in Paradise,* one of the worst of Poe's poems, to the *Raven*, the best of the worst (and all were worst); and the lesser tales to the "popular, perfect" *Gold-Bug* and the *Murders in the Rue Morgue*, which *are* undoubtedly the best. T. S. Eliot's singling out of the *Assignation* should, in justice to Mr. Eliot, be assigned to the three parts snobbism.[13]

Concerning "the pure essence of his locality"—it is gratifying to find Poe avoiding the temptation to exploit theatrical American subjects. But what is "the sullen, volcanic inevitability of the *place*" to be found in Poe? Presumably the essence of this locality should permeate his poems. What is, then, the locality "so coldly nebulous" in his essays, that "luminosity that comes of a dissociation from anything else than the thought and ideals? America's first originality of *place* in literature was, it seems, of Guy de Vere's and Israfel's, of Lenore's and Annabel's in worlds of moon, in haunted palaces, of Eulalies and other girls with eyes of purple tints and pearls, of chambers where the embers were glittering and shining like the cushion's velvet lining, like the velvet violet lining, of filmy Thules where an Eidolon covered green isles and the lakes of Eden and uncovered the drowsy hells in the dells, dells, dells, dells, dells, dells, dells.

About Poe there is
No supernatural mystery-
No extraordinary eccentricity of fate—[14]

One must agree with Dr. Williams in his conclusions. There is no supernatural mystery because Poe was plain and significant—significant because—and this is the only amendment to be made to Dr. Williams' generalization—he was plainly insignificant.

Many apologies may be made for Poe on the ground that, if his sins are the sins of journalism, he was, however, forced into journalism by economic necessity. But Poe never behaved like a man forced into journalism; rather like a man born to journalism and to the least competent and least dignified aspects of journalism. The spirit of journalism vitiated his poems, his formal criticism. It even marred his prose fiction, whose nature admitted of the exercise of a journalistic sense. For Poe was a slipshod, insincere detective: the spring of imaginative invention in him was not disinterested, accurate curiosity, but a desire to produce a certain kind of effect in a reader estimated as having the mean intelligence of the masses. If the sole object of a work is to produce a predetermined effect, then it is bound to be attended by vagueness rather than by particularity. The false atmosphere of Poe's poems are caused by the same devotion to effect as is displayed in the tales. They are both literary rush-orders.

Casting aside all inhibitions of either snobbism or loyalty let us see how Poe, in his two most "popular, perfect" tales, conspicuously betrays himself by revealing this vagueness to be not so much a conscious creative device as a deficiency in mental quality, in *fineness*. Both of these, indeed—they are the *Gold-Bug* and the *Murders in the Rue Morgue*—affect and seem to demand an *effect* of great accuracy. But as it is only the *effect* of accuracy which is demanded and not accuracy itself, inaccuracies and discrepancies appear, covered only by the haste of composition and the indulgence of the unexacting reader, who is taken for granted. Can it be thought that these inaccuracies and discrepancies were purposely introduced as an aid to the *effect* of accuracy? There might be some reason for believing this if Poe had not repeatedly represented himself as a connoisseur of detail. Poe *addressed* the popular taste; but he *defended* himself against a hypothetical enquiring criticism.

The main point on which the Rue Morgue mystery hangs is that it was impossible to discover how the murderer (the ape) got in and out of the room, which was on the fourth story of an old house. The neighbours were at the door and the only ways out were two windows and a chimney. The chimney was too narrow and both windows were closed. Poe tells us that what happened was that the ape came in at one of the two windows by climbing up a lightning-rod. The window was open, yet a large unwieldy bedstead obscured the lower portion, pressed close against it. The only way to open the window from the inside was to stand on the bed and slide the hand down behind the head-board, there pressing a secret spring; a spring so secret that the police had not observed its counterpart in the other window of the room (which was, however, securely shut by a nail hammered through the window-frame). A most improbable arrangement, all round, especially as concerns the existence of such a mechanism in an old, shabby house and on the fourth story. The ape reached the window from the lightning-rod, which was five and a half feet away, by a shutter three and a half feet broad which could shut like a door to cover the whole window and was now lying flat against the wall. He grasped the "trellis-work" on the upper part of the shutter and swung himself into the room, landing unobserved directly on the head of the bed. This is impossible. Poe at one point suggests that it was a double-sashed window: he speaks of the "lower sash." But does not say, whether only the lower sash moved, or both sashes, or whether the two sashes were really one single piece. If only the lower sash moved, then the ape, grasping the shutter and kicking himself backwards (frontways is impossible) into the room, would have been obstructed by the upper half of the window from landing directly on the head of the bed, which was pressed close against the window. If only the lower half moved, then it was only the lower half that was open. If, however, the upper sash moved too, the ape, on climbing out and shutting the window behind him, as he is said to have done, could not have fastened this upper sash by the secret "catch" which was at the bottom of the window and therefore controlling the lower sash. The window would have remained open.

At another point Poe describes "the window" as "dropping upon his exit" and becoming fastened automatically by the catch. This suggests that the window may have been in one piece, hinged at the top with the catch at the bottom, opening upwards and outwards (not inwards because of the bed being in the way). In this case the shutters could not have swung beyond halfway; they would have collided with the window, and again the ape could not have got in. The exact constitution of the window, one of the leading elements of the mystery, remains obscure. There are numerous other falsities in this story: the failure of anyone to find the sailor's pigtail ribbon lying beside the corpse until the detective picked it up a day or so later; the subsequent movements of the ape, which was not seen by anyone in Paris throughout the excitement; the time-factor of the murders.

The *Gold-Bug* similarly does not work out in many points. If the difference of two and a half inches between the two eye-holes of the skull, through one of which the weighted line was to be dropped, made a difference of "several yards" in the final calculation of the buried treasure's position, how was it that the main branch forking from the tree "at a height of some sixty or seventy feet" had not grown enough in the hundred and thirty odd years that had elapsed since the death of Captain Kidd to throw out the measurement by a quarter of a mile? Poe carefully makes the limb growing from the branch dead in order to obscure this: but even supposing the bough to have died the year that the skull was nailed to it, and to have hung dead for all that time, would the branch have stopped growing too? And what natural historic monstrosity was this gold bug, anyhow, of a species totally new, alive and excessively heavy? What part has it in a supposedly rationalistic story?

Such are the methods generally used by Poe, the covering of one obscurity with another, the heaping of aggressive scorn on his puppet police or on his puppet critics and the establishment of a forced confidence in himself by his knowledge of the workings of trick mechanisms and by superfluous quotations from Latin and French. The work and the person of Edgar Allan Poe did not need a sentimental revival or the publication of new material in order to be seen in their proper light. He has been no mystery and nothing pertinent to an understanding of Poe has ever been suppressed, because Poe himself suppressed nothing. He published more than enough to reveal the quality of his mind and of his personality; and he was never obscure. The mystery is not Poe, but how Poe, with all the evidence we have had from the beginning, ever came to be a legitimate literary subject at all with serious readers and still more serious critics. The only solution to be advanced is that the readers are serious and the critics still more serious, but that they cannot have read Poe. The only explanation, indeed, for Poe is that nobody has ever read him. Otherwise it is inconceivable that even the most serious reader and the still more serious critic should be taken in by him.

The steps, however, by which Poe came to occupy this singular position are not difficult to trace. First, that national vanity and academic snobbism in French literary criticism which assumes the burden of making writers of other nations popular to these nations; the constant need in French poetry for new theory by which to live; and the character of Poe's literary criticism, which was not a mature, applied criticism (a mature criticism is never any good to any poetry but its own) but an irrational, noisy rhetoric well suited to bolster up weak literary theorizing. Next, that the uplift of Poe was in another respect accomplished outside the limits of English literary criticism: by students of abnormal psychology to whom Poe furnished an example of eccentric genius rather by his reputed personal habits than by the character of his poetry or of his criticism. Finally, from critical cowardice, came the adoption of Poe by professional criticism itself and by all camps of this criticism. It is another question, who has ever read Poe; that he has managed, as everybody's darling, to pass through the ranks and, arriving in a new day, to raise the standard of Al Aaraaf side by side with that of *The Waste Land* is at least incontestable.

It is first of all important to remove the diæresis from Poe's name and at the same time the sentimental diæresis that dots Poe's life in the eyes of those critics to whom criticism is a form of biographical sympathy. It is certain from the tone of all of Poe's comments on his life, if from nothing else, that his secret and unsatisfied ambition was to be a great autobiographer. Tear away the romance with which the French have surrounded the spelling of his name and the facts of his life; the romantic origin traceable to his Celtic background, where Poe is likewise Poë (and who has not a romantic origin hidden away in his blood somewhere?); and there is left a mediocre but vulgar talent, placed in the less immediate foreground of public attention, seeking to distinguish itself through affected refinements. His morbid preoccupation with autobiographical melodrama prevented Poe from enjoying a serene success even in the minor literary fields for which he was perhaps fitted.

Of his apparently uneventful childish school life in England Poe later wrote in an artificial vein of De Quincey melancholia ("the sad experience of my schoolboy days"); he was never at any time without a Mme de Warens. And whether or not he invented an opportunity for helping the Greeks against "their Turkish tyrants," he was at any rate guilty of many personal Byronisms,[15] such as Byron collars, an overbearing manner and his swim "from Ludlam's wharf to Warwick (six miles) in a hot June sun, against one of the strongest tides ever known in the river." ("The writer," he says in a letter, "seems to compare my swim with that of Lord Byron. . . . Any swimmer 'in the falls' in my days would have swum the Hellespont, and thought nothing of the matter.") The Goethe-Rousseau-Byron-De Quincey autobiographical romanticism with which he later scented his early life was mainly retrospective fiction. He had a dutiful though indifferent foster-father, a sentimental, doting foster-mother, child-loves, early-loves, education, an allowance he considered illiberal and a desire to run away—in other words an exceedingly normal and comfortable early history as early histories go. But partly from inherited dramatic instincts—both his parents had been actors—and partly from the intoxication of authorship in a febrile brain, he was pleased to invent for himself a heroism and a pathos. The pathos carried him through life, the heroism through literature. His life, from his own lips, conveyed passion in conflict with the enemies of passion, mysterious destiny and that atmosphere of spiritual brooding which makes ambition forgivable as the whimsical tail of genius. Unfortunately for Poe, English is a poor language for atmosphere, it is too plain, too suspicious: as a Rimbaud or a Verlaine he was only sham French. Even as a Byron he lacked the easy swagger and generosity of mood proper to truly elevated vulgarity. His literary ambitiousness suggests comparison with Keats. But Keats did not calculate success. He had a haughty enthusiasm for himself, something just a degree beyond vanity, that prevented him from aiming. Poe aimed. He conducted his career like a business-man, he invested in himself. Otherwise miscalculations of taste and sense need not necessarily have meant failure. As it was, one false move would lose him. And as he was all false moves, he had to spend his energy in making them seem consistent with one another, and so to come out right. Undoubtedly every poet, or every person who has ever written poems, has at some time thought of himself as a candidate for fame and thus caused temporary exaggerations in his person and work. Where such exaggerations are due to innocent enthusiasm, they are merely romantic lapses and do not permanently damage the respect, or personal virtue, which should attach to character that is to be remembered. But Poe was consistent and crafty in his exaggerations and therefore unforgivable There is an unclean taint in his personal relationships, which were intense but not serious; in the astuteness with which he devoted himself to athletics, adventure, soldiering and being unhappy—an astuteness without rapture; in the pity with which he always spoke of himself; in the swollen self-consciousness of his prefaces and of the *Marginalia*.

It was not even a monstrous taint, but a small, comtemptible, paranoic one. Poe has been a popular subject of psychological criticism, which is fond of denning genius in terms of abnormality. It is true he had an abnormal passion for greatness, but for greatness of reputation, not greatness of work.

Paranoia, then, was not an unconscious element of Poe's poetic genius, but a wilfully created fiction of persecution and a publicity method. Mr. Allan was an ideal poet's guardian. At the worst, his attitude to Poe may be called "sensible." His idea of his duty to him was to provide him with stable "future prospects." Considering the sentimental intimacy existing between Poe and his wife, he can be forgiven for wanting in affection for him, even for reacting against him if this intimacy was as effusive as all Poe's future ones with women. The illusion of persecution, it may be said, has been common in poets—in Shelley, for example. But in the first place Shelley's family was actively hostile to him; in the second place Shelley had a genuine sense of universal persecution, the obsession of mankind in pain. The weakness of Poe's romantic pessimism is that it concerned no one but himself, and himself in small matters. The difficulties of his life are those of a pushing talent, not of a tragic genius.

With women, especially with older women, Poe's favourite rôle was that of the unhappy and persecuted youth of genius. This inclination for older rather than younger women was a persistent one. It was undoubtedly on Mrs. Clemm's account that he married Virginia: Mrs. Clemm informally succeeded Mr. Allan as guardian when the latter's interest and sense of duty to Poe weakened and when, finally, he entirely neglected him in his will. So Poe combined sentiment and patronage. The fact is, Poe did not like men and did not get on with them. He needed the companionship of women because they pitied him and because their pity did no damage to his dignity—it was merely their tribute to his nobility. Virginia, who as a little girl had carried his love letters, as his wife never interfered with any of Poe's sentimental romances. To her they were "poetical episodes in which the impassioned romance of his temperament impelled him to indulge." Unfortunately most of the objects of Poe's "impassioned romances" did not make suitable heroines of Sentiment; they were respectable women, on too small a scale for the *grande passion*, exercising their maternal instinct and their poetical female fancy on an affected and rather ridiculous young man. However *sympathique* Poe may have been to his poetesses and early and late loves, it is impossible to see him otherwise than as a vain and foolish aspirant, whose real misfortunes, even, seem unreal because he sympathized too much with himself.

Two years after he left West Point Poe won a prize given by *The Saturday Morning Visiter* for the best short story submitted in a competition. Through the publicity gained by this success he made many influential friends and connections with current magazines. In two years he became the editor of the *Southern Literary Messenger*. Before he was twenty-three Poe had published three volumes of poems, the first when he was eighteen. In the preface to this he claims most of them to have been written before the completion of his fourteenth year; and its style reveals, indeed, the self-appointed child of genius making his first disdainful bow to the public.

> They were not of course intended for publication; why they are now published concerns no one but himself. . . . In "Tamerlane" he has endeavoured to expose the folly of even *risking* the best feelings of the heart at the shrine of Ambition. . . . There are many faults . . . which he flatters himself he could, with little trouble, have corrected, but unlike many of his predecessors, has been too fond of his early productions to amend them in his *old age*.
>
> He will not say that he is indifferent to the success of these Poems—it might stimulate him to other attempts—but he can safely say that failure will not influence him in a resolution already adopted. This is challenging criticism—let it be so. "Nos haec novimus esse nihil."[16]

The theme of nearly all of these early poems of Poe's is thwarted Power. The "cold reality of waking life" Poe knew before he had awakened, by temperamental premonition: he was *born* saying "I *have been* happy, Tho' in a dream." Tamerlane is his Childe Harold. In the 1829 edition he shortened the poem, but made it, if anything, even more unabashed than the excited but rather ingenuous original.

An examination of Byron's first literary confession, his preface to *Hours of Idleness*, will best show the class into which Poe's adolescent snobbery falls. This preface is preceded by quotations from Horace, Homer and Dryden and continues as follows:

> TO THE RIGHT HONOURABLE
> FREDERICK, EARL OF CARLISLE
> KNIGHT OF THE GARTER ETC. ETC.,
> THE SECOND EDITION OF THESE POEMS IS INSCRIBED
> BY HIS
> OBLIGED AND AFFECTIONATE KINSMAN
> THE AUTHOR
>
> In submitting to the public eye the following collection, I have not only to combat the difficulties writers of verse generally encounter, but may incur the charge of presumption for obtruding myself on the world, when, without doubt, I might be, at my age, more usefully employed.

> These productions are the fruits of the lighter hours of a young man who has lately completed his nineteenth year. As they bear the internal evidence of a boyish mind, this is perhaps unnecessary information. . . . I am sensible that the partial and frequently injudicial admiration of a social circle is not the criterion by which poetical genius is to be estimated. . . . Poetry, however, is not my primary vocation; to divert the dull moments of indisposition, or the monotony of a vacant hour, urged me 'to this sin': little can be expected of so unpromising a muse.
>
> [Here follows a sardonic reference to the 'genuine' bards.]
>
> With slight hopes, and some fears, I publish this first and last attempt. . . . The opinion of Dr. Johnson, on the Poems of a noble relation of mine,* 'that when a man of rank appeared in the character of an author, he deserved to have his merit handsomely allowed,' can have little weight with verbal, and still less with periodical censors; but were it otherwise, I should be loth to avail myself of the privilege, and would rather incur the bitterest censure of anonymous criticism, than triumph in honours granted solely to a title.[17]

Poe's second publication of poems owned the conspicuously suppressed authorship of the first "By a Bostonian" and offered the gratuitous information that this was "suppressed through circumstances of a private nature." The first was without dedication, the second bore two dedications, a formal literary dedication

> Who drinks the deepest?—here's to him.—
>
> Cleveland;

and a personal dedication of *Tamerlane* to John Neal, Editor of the *Yankee*, the first of the long suite of editors and persons of literary influences whom Poe so frantically pursued during his whole lifetime. To the theme of the first volume, thwarted power, this volume added the minor vein of renunciatory solitude.

Poe's third volume, formally dedicated to the U.S. Corps of Cadets, was published in the same year that he obtained his dismissal from the West Point Military Academy. The literary quotation on the title page this time reads "Tout le monde a Raison.—Rochefoucault." It is accompanied by an elaborate preface in the form of a letter to Mr.—. It includes an ingenious

*Frederick Howard, fifth Earl of Carlisle, author of fugitive pieces and two tragedies, was born 1748, and died in 1826.—Author

defence of a poet's good opinion of his own work; an impassioned refutation of the Lake School as making poetry so removed from popular understanding as to rob it of pleasure; a special trouncing of Wordsworth; a partial pleading for Coleridge; and a formal definition of poetry in reference to science, romance, music and prose. This is a specimen of Poe's prefatorial manner: "Think of poetry, dear B—Think of poetry and then think of—Dr. Samuel Johnson! Think of all that is airy and fairy-like, and then of all that is hideous and unwieldy: think of his huge bulk, the Elephant! and then—and then think of the Tempest—the Midsummer Night's Dream—Prospero—Oberon—and Titania!" It is clear from these early writings that Poe's professional arrogance and violence must not be laid to alcoholism. The more we learn about Poe, the more grateful we are for his alcoholism. It was apparently the one thing that could restrain Poe from himself: the idea of a sober Poe is intolerable.

The impression to be got from everything written by Poe is that it was meant to be read immediately, that its design was a spontaneous and gratifying effect; that is, his creative direction was always journalistic. Indeed Poe wasted the best part of his energy in editing and writing for magazines and in trying to found one of his own. It is Poe's passion for journalism that prevented him from ever reaching maturity in his art and in his criticism; and the literary uses to which he put journalism that prevented him from attaining any dignity as a journalist.

The constant agitation in which Poe is found, his unashamed solicitation of approval, his rash exercise of critical vanity in place of critical judgment, all this makes the picture of an Effort conniving at too great an Aim and therefore driven to practice certain violences and delusions on itself. The intensity of Poe's campaign for greatness is shown by the way in which a portion of posterity has succumbed to it. Poe had a terrible suspicion of success in others; everywhere he looked he seemed to see a need for self-justification. The result was the pompous and childish disdain with which he wrote of the Literati: "Some honest opinions about authorial merits and demerits, with occasional words of Personality"; and the note of false ease and self-confidence in which he couched his more regular compositions.

The *Marginalia* in particular (originally newspaper book-chat) give evidence of Poe's nervousness, his desire to achieve a natural manner through journalism. In these, by writing as casually as he knew how, he hoped to prove himself at home in literature. The futile sarcasm of these notes, their showiness in strained and overworked literary references, expose his greatest weakness, his inability to be off-hand. His desire in them was to exercise wit and opinion without the restraint imposed by more formal journalistic channels, to enjoy in public the privilege of private ranting. They are full of examples of the perversion of taste by journalism: his attachment to journalism itself ("I will not be sure that men at present think more profoundly than half a century ago, but beyond question they think with more rapidity, with more skill, with more tact, with more of method and less of excrescence in the thought. Besides all this they have a vast increase in the thinking material, they have more facts, more to think about. For this reason they are disposed to put the greatest amount of thought in the smallest compass and disperse it with the utmost attainable rapidity. Hence the journalism of the age; hence, in especial, magazines. Too many we cannot have, as a general proposition."); his tribute to Thomas Moore (this was just before Moore had "gone out") and Tennyson, "the greatest of poets"; his disproportionate interest in Dickens and the criticism of Dickens; technical appreciations of Longfellow; an ill-tempered and uneasy weakness for Ossian, echoing his condemnation of Wordsworth, in an early preface, for his "absurdity" in attempting to prove the worthlessness of these poems ("But worse still:"—to quote from this preface—"that he [Wordsworth] may beat down every argument in favour of these poems, he triumphantly drags forward a passage, in his abomination of which he expects the reader to sympathize. It is the beginning of the epic poem 'Temora.' 'The blue waves of Ullin roll in light; the green hills are covered with day; trees shake their dusky heads in the breeze.' And this—this gorgeous, yet simple imagery—where all is alive and panting with immortality—than which earth has nothing more grand, nor paradise more beautiful—this William Wordsworth, the author of 'Peter Bell,' has *selected* to dignify with his supreme contempt").

Much of Poe's critical irritability was undoubtedly due to his private awareness of his errors of taste. Obviously sentiment and taste were in conflict in him and he formed his judgments by allowing sentiment to rule taste; without, however, being willing to admit the total defeat of taste. The truth is that Poe had an equal capacity for the right and the wrong in literature, but a morbid perversity by which he could not resist the temptation to his pride to go wrong. And in defending his errors Poe defended his sentiment, never his taste. He is never at rest, he is continually visualizing himself as the protagonist of a drama in which he is the defender of an unpopular but noble sentiment, or inventing "good ideas for a Magazine paper," whether it is to show how "a modest young gentleman" gets the better in an argument of "a flippant pretender to universal acquirement" or how a particular poem attained its ultimate point of completion. "Why such a paper has never been given to the world, I am much at a loss to say—but perhaps the authorial vanity has more to do with the omission than any one other cause." And so

Poe sets about to write such a paper on the construction of *The Raven* to flout popular superstitions about authorial vanity and the mysteriousness with which the processes of creation are supposed to be surrounded, describing a poetic method for *The Raven* most likely to antagonize popular superstition.[18] This mechanical recipe-method, by the way, is apparently contrary to the actual facts of the case. For according to the two stories of its composition circulated by unprejudiced personal gossip, more acceptable than Poe's too neat, too glib mathematical scheme for the poem (unless Poe meant his own story to be understood as a critical joke, which is unlikely), the poem was either "dashed off" one evening after a long walk at Poe's most gloomy period, when Virginia was on her deathbed and the family starving, or its composition covered a longer period, being written in instalments, passed round among his friends over and over again for criticism, altered, rewritten, juggled into shape: whichever of these two may be true, nevertheless constructed along any but systematic lines.

Poe's egotism was so extremely sensitive that it was always expressed as a defence of his offensiveness, not of his greatness: he had a superstitious faith in opposition and therefore a martyr's love of *insult*. When accused of madness he could make no definite reply but a categorical defence of madness: "The question is not yet settled whether madness is or is not the loftiest intelligence, whether much that is glorious, whether all that is profound, does not spring from diseases of thought—from *moods* of mind exalted at the expense of the general intellect." In this manner Poe laid the foundations for the myth of genius via abnormality by which he was subsequently ennobled in literary history. "Why, to be frank," he says in the *Gold-Bug*, "I felt somewhat annoyed by your evident suspicions touching my sanity, and so resolved to punish you quietly, in my own way, by a little bit of sober mystification." In the preface of the 1845 edition of his poems, dedicated to Elizabeth Barrett Barret, "the noblest of her sex," appears just such another scornful statement of a principle he knew would be inacceptable to the critical public. In defending himself from this public he removes all possibility of critical sympathy by defining his poetry as a passion, not as a purpose (a way of stating his indifference "to the paltry commendations of mankind" calculated to prove most obnoxious to mankind), and by concluding with the sweeping generalization that "the passions must be held in reverence." He behaved as if, his case being hopeless with criticism, he was free to yield to his temperament and use the manner of a private diary.

But Poe's personal arrogance about his work is one matter and the work another and his critical writing still another. The private diarist is protecting himself from failure by haughtily anticipating failure. The author of the work is protecting himself from failure by making neat calculations on the side in the science of popular taste. The critic is protecting himself from the possible vulgar success of the author by trying to establish that vulgar success can also be literary success. So the critic and the private diarist are reconciled, since the failure of the diarist meant, of course, only vulgar failure. The vulgar success of Poe's poems was elevated into formal literary success in two ways. They have obviously that lack of distinction and that facility of sentiment which are the two requirements for acceptable magazine verse—poetry, that is, which neither has nor desires a passport to criticism. But since these magazine successes, these little recitation classics, are the result of a design, a journalist's careful measurement of how far surface-emotions of the reader may be taken, the design in itself is criticism. Poe thus made criticism of his poems and poems of his criticism, and they have conferred on each other a mutual distinction, in both cases an acquired one. The second formal corroboration of the vulgar success of Poe's poems is of an accidental nature: that by their technical musicalness and sense-combining effects they happen to appeal to those pianoforte experimentalists in French poetry who are always trying to achieve the surface purity which music and painting, for example, are thought to have. Perhaps more than half of Poe's literary respectability is just such back-door respectability.

His criticism, indeed, cannot be estimated except as part of his personal system. It is constantly cancelling itself in anti-climaxes; as the generalities of ambition in Poe's temperament are never matched by particular potentialities. His campaign against the long poem, for example, is really only a denunciation of its commercial unreadableness. The interest-value of the poem is at the bottom of all of Poe's critical writing. The contemporary success of a poem is its selling-power; and in his criticism he could discuss this interest-value without violating the professed indifference to success of the private diarist. All of his suppressed anxiety to please comes out in his essays in the guise of critical theory. And as music is the art which concerns itself most with the problem of co-ordinating its technique with the impressionability of the audience, it becomes the analogy on which his construction of the poem is based. His poetic absolute, therefore—"the poem written solely for the poem's sake"—reveals itself as the duty of a poem to give nothing but pleasure; pleasure being further qualified as the "thrill" which poetry communicates by the taint of sadness, the finger-mark of Beauty. Beauty was exemplified in the works of Willis, Longfellow, Bryant, Edward C. Pinkney, Byron, Thomas Moore (who not so far back had visited America and condoled with those Americans who were moved by his pity to confide in him their disappointment

that the powerful stream
Of America's empire should pass like a dream,
Without leaving one relic of genius . . .),[19]

Thomas Hood, Tennyson.

We can get a truer picture of Poe as a critical mind by comparing him with Shelley, another sentimental theorist, rather than by looking at him through the eyes of that advanced criticism which, perhaps because of its subservience to French literary tastes, has condescendingly opened the pearly gates to him. Both Poe and Shelley fixed on Love as the underlying human principle of poetic Beauty. Shelley's explanation of this principle is:

> Poetry lifts the veil from the hidden beauty of the world, and makes familiar objects be as if they were not familiar; it reproduces all that it represents, and the impersonations clothed in its Elysian light stand thenceforward in the minds of those who have once contemplated them, as memorials of that gentle and exalted content which extends itself over all thoughts and actions with which it coexists. The great secret of morals is love; or a going out of our nature, and an identification of ourselves with the beautiful which exists in thought, action, or person, not our own. A man, to be greatly good, must imagine intensely and comprehensively; he must put himself in the place of another and of many others; the pains and pleasures of his species must become his own. The great instrument of moral good is the imagination; and poetry ministers to the effect by acting upon the cause. Poetry enlarges the circumference of the imagination by replenishing it with thoughts of ever new delight, which have the power of attracting and assimilating to their own nature all other thoughts, and which form new intervals and interstices whose void forever craves fresh food.[20]

And Poe's:

> —Love—the true, the divine Eros—the Uranian, as distinguished from the Dionaean Venus—is unquestionably the purest and truest of all poetic themes . . . we shall reach, however, more immediately a distinct conception of what true Poetry is, by mere reference to a few of the simple elements which induce in the Poet himself the true poetical effect. He recognizes the ambrosia which nourishes his soul, in the bright orbs that shine in Heaven—in the volutes of the flower—in the clustering of low shrubberies—in the waving of the grain-fields—in

the slanting of tall Eastern trees—in the blue distance of mountains—in the grouping of clouds—in the twinkling of half-hidden brooks—in the gleaming of silver rivers—in the repose of sequestered lakes—in the star-mirroring depths of lonely wells. He perceives it in the songs of birds—in the harp of Aeolus—in the sighing of the night-wind—in the repining voice of the forest—in the surf that complains to the shore—in the fresh breath of the woods—in the scent of the violet-in the voluptuous perfume of the hyacinth—in the suggestive odour that comes to him, at eventide, from far-distant, undiscovered islands, over dim oceans, illimitable and unexplored. He owns it in all noble thoughts—in all unworldly motives—in all holy impulses—in all chivalrous, generous, and self-sacrificing deeds. He feels it in the beauty of woman—in the grace of her step—in the lustre of her eye—in her sigh—in the harmony of the rustling of her robes. He deeply feels it in her winning endearments—in her burning enthusiasms—in her gentle charities—in her meek and devotional endurances—but above all—ah, far above all—he kneels to it—he worships it in the faith, in the purity, in the strength, in the altogether divine majesty—of her *love.*[21]

The essay from which this is taken closes with a mock-antique poem in illustration of this principle, "The Song of the Cavalier" by William Motherwell, who was Editor of the *Paisley Advertiser* and later of the *Glasgow Courier*, a fellow-journalist.

Then mounte! then mounte, brave gallants, all, And don your helms amaine!" etc.[22]

Let the advanced critic now, to whom Poe is a tribal watchword and Shelley an outcast because he was not literary, swallow this and see whether he can keep it down. Shelley had too earnest a social sense and his poetry suffers from his sympathies. But it is not difficult to keep Shelley down: he does harm to no advocate's dignity. If Shelley had not been over-affected by the ugliness of human society he would have been great—Shelley was momently too unhappy to be great. And perhaps this is as it should be, if he meant to preserve a sort of non-literary human integrity: there is always a certain meanness in greatness. Whatever may have happened to Shelley's poetry, Shelley himself remained true; while Keats, of whom Poe is a cheaper edition, grew too literary to be true. Poe, that is, is cockney, though he never realized this, masquerading as true because he thought himself unhappy—Poe always had a tear in his pocket, as Keats a sigh in his handkerchief. They are both, however, seen as upholders of a Taste which Shelley is thought to have violated, because neither of them had power to do more than put forward their personal claims to fame.

"I prefer commencing with the consideration of an *effect*," boasts Poe, having once decided that "*a*" poem must be written which shall "suit at once the popular and the critical taste"—we are given no clue as to which is which.[23] Deeply conscious of the fact that his own limitations forced him to oppose virtuosity to genius, Poe was always brazenly on the defensive in discussing poetic technique. Real poetry (poetry that was a passion not a purpose!), he convinced himself, was always written by rhythm and rote. Indeed an "interesting magazine paper might be written by any author who would . . ." etc. It was a shame-complex that drove Poe to the exhibitionism of his analysis of the *Raven*—of which he was probably, because of its history, most ashamed. The recipe for the ideal poem to be deduced from this analysis is:

1. A one-sitting length (about 100 lines).
2. Elevation and excitement.
3. Universal appeal.
4. Beauty (not Truth or Passion)—"Truth demands a precision, and Passion a *homeliness*, which are absolutely antagonistic to that *Beauty* which, I maintain, is the excitement, or pleasurable elevation, of the soul."
5. Melancholy—"Melancholy is the most legitimate of all poetical tones."
6. "Artistic poignancy"—"*points*, in the theatrical sense"—in the *Raven* the refrain, in various combinations, performs this function.
7. Finding the refrain—take *o* and *r* and it is "absolutely impossible to overlook the word 'Nevermore'"!
8. Now find "a pretext" for using the refrain. "A parrot"? No, "a Raven—it is infinitely more in keeping with the *tone*."
9. Choosing the subject—"'Of all melancholy topics, what, according to the *universal* understanding of mankind, is the *most* melancholy?' Death—was the obvious reply."
10. Getting together the scenery—"'And when,' I said, 'is this most melancholy of topics most poetical? When it most closely allies itself to *Beauty*: the death, then, of a beautiful woman is, unquestionably, the most poetical topic in the world—and equally is it beyond doubt that the lips best suited for such topic are those of a bereaved lover.'"

With these few simple precautions, the rest is easy, "the ominous reputation of the fowl" will carry it through. Of course, write the first stanza last, and work backward until the hundred (or hundred and eight) lines are used up, "enfeebling" them as the beginning is neared to preserve the "climacteric effect" of the last. And of course, a little originality in rhythm and metre. Then put the lover in a room, "*a close circumscription of space*" to make all cosy, and let in the fowl, who alights on a bust of Pallas, "chosen, first, as most in keeping with the scholarship of the lover, and, secondly, for the sonorousness of the word Pallas itself. With an "indulgence, to the extreme, of self-torture" and an eye to the "artistical eye" and a few minor considerations having chiefly to do with sauce, the poem is done to a turn.

Such is the philosophy of composition and such the theorist who has contributed so much to the science of modern French verse. Recently Valéry's translator, Mr. Malcolm Cowley, quoted from his translation of *Variété* the following:

> What critics call a *realization*, or a successful rendering, is really a problem of efficiency . . . in which the only factors are the nature of the material and the mentality of the public. Edgar Allan Poe . . . has clearly established his appeal to the reader on the basis of psychology and probable effect.
>
> The most important ingredient of literary composition is the idea of *the most probable reader*. . . . The change of century, which means a change of reader, is comparable to an alteration in the text itself.[24]

Adding himself the never-failing analogy: "The poem is conceivably, the pearl certainly, the result of an unhealthy condition. But this has nothing whatever to do with their own *effects*." The poem, by excessive analogy—criticism's last resort—with pictures, symphonies, pearls and other consumable products, ceases to be production. What Valéry calls "the problem of efficiency" is the elimination of production. Consumption is production. Demand is supply. Poet is public. Poet is a dud.

Even Mr. Eliot sandwiches Poe between Donne and Mallarmé as a *metaphysical* poet, treating the problem of Poe's effects and his methods of achieving them with apparent seriousness.[25] (Poe is to be tolerated in this position if only to separate Donne from Mallarmé.) Yet Poe's contributions to the theory of verse amounted to no more than a bombastic attack on the prosodists, to prove that the alternation of syllables in verse was *not* regular; a theory that all life began with the spondee; and all that false technical association of verse with music ("*verse*, an inferior or less capable music"[26]) which is found to be of service and self-gratification to criticism when the life-blood of poetry has run low and criticism is looking for a "science" by which it may be restored.

And who are Poe's references or authorities in his indignant rationale of verse? Mr. N. P. Willis, author of "such lines" as

> That binds him to a woman's delicate love—

"but one of the innumerable instances he has given of keen sensibility in all those matters of taste which may be classed under the general head of *fanciful* embellishment; Mr. Horne (of England), the author of 'Orion,' one of the noblest epics in any language"; Edgar Allan Poe, in "Al Aaraaf, a boyish poem written by myself when a boy" in which occur "two *consecutive* equivalent feet"—"I cannot say I have ever known the adventure made" (except here)—equivalent, "that is to say, feet the sum of whose syllabic time is equal to the sum of the syllabic times of the distinctive feet"; "one of the finest poets, Mr. Christopher Pease Branch,[27] who begins a very beautiful poem thus":

> Many are the thoughts that come to me
> In my lonely musing:

Mrs. Welby, author of "a little poem of great beauty" containing a "variable foot":

> I have a little stepson of only three years old.

Miss Mary A. S. Aldrich, author of "quite a pretty specimen of verse":

> The water lily sleeps in pride
> Down in the depths of the azure lake.

One would like to pity Poe, if possible, as he wished, but his appeals for pity were so undignified that it is scarcely dignified to pity him. One would like to sympathize with him in his outspoken and fierce attacks on contemporary criticism and pedantry—there is no doubt Poe lived in one of the worst of times for literature. But they have a bad grace and an overweeningness that harm the attacker rather than the attacked. His wit was warped and thinned out by petty ambitioning; and whatever our feelings may be about the *North American Review* as it was in Poe's time, we are not amused when Poe suggests that it be thrown to the pigs.

Poe was only satiric when he lost his temper, and as he was continually losing his temper he could not be satiric with much conviction. He was always losing his temper because he was always looking for the ideal public.

The ideal public was one which could immediately appreciate his work, which was ideal for the ideal public. He knew what the ideal public was, but it was apparently as slow as it was ideal. It was not the false sales public, nor the clique public. It was, it seems, that "not-too-acute reader," as he called him in his review of *Barnaby Rudge*, that "excitable, undisciplined and child-like popular mind which most keenly feels the original," as he called him in his review of *Twice Told Tales*. The fault, indeed, he had to find with Hawthorne was that he was not original, only "peculiar," that is, he did not make use of that technique of which *effect* is the sole object and in which new and "pleasurable" emotions are aroused through the mechanism of mystery. Poe, in his praise of originality, excluded those who "limited the literary to the metaphysical originality." (How does this tally with Mr. Eliot's classification of Poe as metaphysical?) Metaphysical originality, Poe claimed, offended the masses because, by seeking absolute novelty of combination, it resembled instruction.—"True originality . . . combines with the pleasurable effect of *apparent* novelty, a real egotistic delight." Hawthorne, by his charm and fancifulness, shared in this true originality, but in a lesser degree, not so much because his allegory was false as because it was "removed from the popular intellect, from the popular sentiment, and from the popular taste." Allegory was too close to truthfulness—it cannot be too strongly emphasized that to Poe the essence of composition was fictitiousness designed to produce an *effect*. This is why he evoked music in support and this is why he glorified the mystery-story and the mystery-poem—the petty journalist's contribution to the problem of reconciling the rough reading masses to the fine writers. The poem and the tale were to him the two complementary acts of creation, the poem being obliged to use "artificialities" of rhythm to bring out "the idea of the Beautiful" which were "an inseparable bar" to "Truth," the tale being able to make use of elements "(the ratiocinative, the sarcastic or the humorous) which are not only antagonistical to the nature of the poem, but absolutely forbidden by one of its most peculiar and indispensable adjuncts; we allude, of course, to rhythm."

It is a sad picture, a gloomy and sentimental hack, seeing plagiarism of himself everywhere because his own poor capacities for melodrama naturally produced the same results as other poor capacities; plotting mystery tales, plotting mystery poems, solving conjuror's tricks; constructing feeble ladyships and creaking phantoms; triumphantly checking the plot errors in long, dull Victorian serial stories; thinking up "good ideas" for Magazine articles. The solution seems to be to leave him to the romantic esteem of the French, who are so eminently qualified to sympathize with (ah!) "les beaux cris de passion sincère, les beaux élans d'amour,"[28] as his French translator,

M. Gabriel Mourey, calls them; to receive in tender immortality the many who were Poe's only loves and to place him among the candidates for pity in whom their own literary history is so rich. "Baudelaire, Mallarmé, Hennequin, Rollinat, vous-même d'autres encore . . ."[29] (Rimbaud and Verlaine we might add) "on a tant fait en France pour y acclimater Edgar Poe que ses compatriotes affirment que l'auteur du *Corbeau* était francais," wrote John H. Ingram, Poe's most inspired advocate to Poe's French translator.[30] One leading clue to Poe's French reputation seems to be that "Poe aimait la France et son admirable littérature et ne parlait qu'avec respect des chefs-d'œuvre qu'elle a produits; jamais sa plume caustique ne serait essayer à diminuer sa gloire."[31] Another is that by the antagonism his personality left behind him, he could be used as an effective scourge against the "philistins." Poe's chief adaptability to the French temper, however, must lie in the infinite advantage any inferior work has when translated into French, a language whose large sonorousness and refined daintiness supplies to Poe's poems just that element of musical "fugitiveness" which the English language is more strict in refusing to yield.

> "Prophète" dis-je, "créature du mal!—Prophète cependant, oiseau ou démon !—
> Soit le Tentateur t'ait mandé ou soit que la Tempête t'ait rejeté sur ce rivage,
> Désolé, mais indompté, sur cette terre déserte enchantée.
> Sur ce foyer hauté par l'Horreur—dis-moi, vraiment, je t'implore—
> Y a-t-il, *-y a-t-il* un baume dans Galaad? Dis-moi—dis-mois, je t'implore!"
> Fit le Corbeau: "Jamais plus."[32]

A few internal rhymes may, of course, be lost in the translation, but Poe would undoubtedly have remedied this deficiency if he had written the poem originally in French himself.

One mystery remains, the popularity of Poe with that portion of critical opinion which should, by all sense and taste, disregard him most. Why, indeed, should Mr. Eliot share with the French their particular admiration for the tale called the *Assignation*? Because of the poetical motto from Henry King's (Bishop of Chichester) *Exequy On The Death Of His Wife*, and because Mr. Eliot has more than a weakness for poetical mottoes? Because of the Venetian setting and because Venice is romantically situated in the international cosmography of Mr. Eliot's mind? Because of the literary references to Socrates, Michelangelo, Chapman and others included in a tale often and a half pages, and because Mr. Eliot has more than a weakness for literary references? He cannot surely be serious in advancing that Poe makes the most artificial melodrama seem real, with this tale in particular—one of the most nonsensical—as evidence? Is it to be suggested that this partiality for Poe is a confession of that love of "magnificent meditation," that morbid taste for desolation and ill-fatedness which is more appropriate to the boyish, melodramatic enthusiasm of the penny dreadfuls than to advanced contemporary poetry and criticism—unless these are willing to confess to internal melodrama, as they apparently are not?

Editors' Notes

Chapter 1 Poetry and the Literary Universe

1. The opening chapter of *Contemporaries and Snobs* presents the main argument of the book, and was never published elsewhere. Riding likely wrote much of it in 1926 and 1927, in response to a few works of recent criticism, including Edith Sitwell's *Poetry and Criticism* (London: Hogarth Press, 1925); Edwin Muir's *Transition: Essays on Contemporary Literature* (London: Hogarth Press, 1926); the October 1926 issue of Eliot's journal, the *New Criterion*; and Allen Tate's "Poetry and the Absolute," which Riding read in draft form [Laura (Riding) Jackson and Schuyler B. Jackson collection, #4608, Division of Rare and Manuscript Collections, Cornell University Library, Series IX, Box 100, folder 3] though it later appeared in the January 1927 issue of *The Sewanee Review*. After Leonard and Virginia Woolf declined to publish *Contemporaries* at Hogarth Press, Riding offered this opening essay to Wyndham Lewis for publication in his journal, *The Enemy*, but Lewis also turned it down [Friedmann, Elizabeth. *A Mannered Grace: The Life of Laura Riding Jackson* (New York: Persea, 2005), 114–116].

2. Arthur Rimbaud, letter to Paul Demeny, May 15, 1871. In this letter appears the famous statement, "Car je est un autre" ("I is an other/I am an other"). The impact of this statement on the development of modernist impersonality cannot be underestimated. Rimbaud attempts to explain how the poet distances himself from the subject, how language takes precedence over ego:

> Je dis qu'il faut être voyant, se faire voyant.
>
> Le Poète se fait voyant par un long, immense et raisonné dérèglement de tous les sens. Tous les formes d'amour, de souffrance, de folie; il cherche lui-même, il épuise en lui tous les poisons, pour n'en garder que les quintessences. Ineffable torture où il a besoin de toute la foi, de toute la force

surhumaine, ou il devient entre tous le grand malade, le grand criminel, le grand maudit—et le suprême Savant!

I say that one must be a seer, make oneself a seer.

The Poet makes himself a seer by an immense, slow, and intentional disordering of all the senses. All the forms of love, suffering, and insanity; he searches himself, he rids himself of all poisons and keeps only the quintessence. An ineffable and torturous process for which he needs complete faith, superhuman strength, and from it he becomes the diseased, the criminal, the damned—and the supreme scholar!

3. Percy Bysshe Shelley, "A Defense of Poetry" (1821).

4. Albert Einstein's *Relativity: The Special and General Theory* was first published in German in 1916 and translated into English by Robert W. Lawson in 1920 (New York: Henry Holt).

5. T. S. Eliot, "Gerontion" (1920).

6. T. S. Eliot, *The Waste Land* (1922). These lines of the poem borrow from Charles Baudelaire's "The Seven Old Men," from *Les Fleurs du Mal* (1857).

7. See Edwin Muir, *Transition: Essays on Contemporary Literature* (London: Hogarth Press, 1926), particularly "Introductory: The Zeit Geist" and the chapters on T. S. Eliot, Edith Sitwell, and Robert Graves, and Edwin Muir's *Chorus of the Newly Dead* (London: Hogarth Press, 1926).

8. Riding is perhaps misremembering Dryden's claim, in the introduction to *Annus Mirabilis* (1667) that "the composition of all poems is, or ought to be, of wit."

9. John Lyly, *Euphues: The Anatomy of Wit* (1578). The full sentence reads, "Englishmen desire to heare finer speech than the language will allow."

10. Samuel Johnson, "The Life of Cowley," *Lives of the Poets* (1779–81).

11. "The Life of Cowley." The full sentence reads, "But Pope's account of wit is undoubtedly erroneous: he depresses it below its natural dignity, and reduces it from strength of thought to happiness of language."

12. Riding came to know Ransom when she was a member of the Fugitive group in the early 1920s. By the time *Contemporaries* was published, Ransom had published three volumes of poetry: *Poems about God* (1919), *Chills and Fever* (1924), and *Two Gentlemen in Bonds* (1927).

13. Erasmus Darwin, *The Botanic Garden* (1791).

14. Riding likely drew her title for this section from Allen Tate's "Poetry and the Absolute." Tate sent Riding this essay in typescript [Laura (Riding) Jackson and Schuyler B. Jackson collection, #4608, Division of Rare and Manuscript Collections, Cornell University Library, Series IX, Box 100, folder 3], and it later ap-

peared in *The Sewanee Review* 35.1 (January 1927): 41–52. In "The Poetic Absolute," Riding argues against Tate's attempt to provide a philosophical basis for a poetic "absolute."

15. Riding met and befriended Hart Crane in New York in 1925. She ceaselessly championed his poetry; her review of Crane's *White Buildings* appeared in *transition* in January 1928 ("A Note on White Buildings," *transition* 10, 139–141).

16. Arthur Rimbaud, letter to Paul Demeny, May 15, 1871. See note 2.

17. Paul Valéry, *Variété II* (Paris: Gallimard, 1929), 28. The full passage reads:

> L'homme des foules est poète, conteur, ou quelque ivrogne de l'esprit. Il se noie dans la quantité des âmes ambulantes; il s'enivre d'absorber un nombre inépuisable de visages et de regards, et de ressentir au fil de la rue fluide le vertige du passage de l'infinité des individus.
>
> The man of the crowd is a poet, a storyteller, or a kind of drunken spirit. He drowns himself in a sea of restless souls; he becomes drunk soaking in an unending sea of faces and looks and, in the wake of the moving streets, experiences vertigo from becoming part of this infinity of individuals.

18. Jean Cocteau, "Lettre à Jacques Maritain." See Jacques and Raïssa Maritain, *Oeuvres complètes, Volume 3* (Atlanta: International Book Center of Atlanta, 1985), 692. The full passage reads:

> J'apprendrai que le besoin de changer en art n'est pas autre chose que celui de chercher une place fraîche sur l'oreiller. Posez la main sure une fraîcheur, elle cesse vite de l'être; le neuf est une fraîcher. Le besoin de neuf est le besoin de fraîcheur. Dieu est la seule fraîcheur qui ne se rechauffe pas.
>
> J'apprendrai à fabriquer les poèmes (le mot est de La Fontaine) et pour le reste à laisser faire Dieu.
>
> I will learn that, in art, the need to change is nothing other than the desire to find a cool place on the pillow to rest one's head. Place the hand on this cool spot, and it quickly ceases to be so; newness is this coolness and freshness. The need to be new is the need for this freshness. God is the only cool spot that never warms to the touch.
>
> I will learn to *make* poems (the word is from La Fontaine) and leave the rest to God.

19. Cocteau, "Lettre à Jacques Maritain." The quote reads: "Imagine, my dear Jacques, the joy of a language free from Rimbaud (right now more cumbersome than Hugo) and from the superstition of Maldoror. All youth could breathe again."

20. "A Brief Treatise on the Criticism of Poetry," *Chapbook* 2.9 (March 1920): 1.

21. "A Brief Treatise on the Criticism of Poetry," *Chapbook* 2.9 (March 1920): 3.

22. "Books of the Quarter" [review of Herbert Read, *Reason and Romanticism: Essays in Literary Criticism* (Faber & Gwyer) and Ramon Fernandez, *Messages* (Paris: Gallimard)] *New Criterion* 4.4 (October 1926): 751.

23. *Naked Warriors* (London: Art and Letters, 1919). The lines read, "Judas no doubt was right / In a mental sort of way: / For he betrayed another and so / With purpose was self-justified."

24. "Books of the Quarter," 751.

25. "Books of the Quarter," 751. The full quotation reads: "Both [Herbert Read and Ramon Fernandez], instead of taking for granted the place and function of literature—and therefore taking for granted a whole universe—are occupied with the inquiry into this function, and therefore with the inquiry into the whole moral world, fundamentally, with entities and values."

26. "Books of the Quarter," 751–2. Eliot writes that "we have from these two writers [Herbert Read and Ramon Fernandez] almost incorrigible testimony to the actual lack of value of Proust, or more exactly, to his value simply as a milestone, as a point of demarcation between a generation for whom the dissolution of value had in itself a positive value, and the generation for which the recognition of value is of utmost importance, a generation which is beginning to turn its attention to an athleticism, a training, of the soul as severe and ascetic as the training of the body of a runner."

27. C. H. Rickword, "Scrutinies (5): Bernard Shaw," *Calendar of Modern Letters* 1.6 (September 1925): 50–54.

28. "Final Confessions—Literary Tests," *Specimen Days* (1892).

29. *Poetry and Criticism* (London: Hogarth Press, 1925), 16. Interestingly, Sitwell draws on the concept of "texture" elaborated by "my friend Mr. Robert Graves" to praise Pope's *The Rape of the Lock* (15).

30. *Poetry and Criticism,* 17.

31. "The Subject-Matter of Poetry," *The Chapbook*, 9 (March 1920): 11–16.

32. Riding is perhaps thinking here of the following lines from Francis Thompson's *Shelley: An Essay* (1909): "It is this gift of not merely embodying but apprehending everything in figure which co-operates towards creating his rarest characteristics, so almost preternaturally developed in no other poet, namely, his well-known power to condense the most hydrogenic abstraction. Science can now educe threads of such exquisite tenuity that only the feet of the tiniest infant-spiders can ascend them; but up the filmiest insubstantiality Shelley runs with agile ease. To him, in truth, nothing is abstract."

33. Riding's parenthetical on Hulme here prefigures her broader treatment of Hulme in Chapter 2. (See chap. 2, n. 6.)

34. *Transition: Essays on Contemporary Literature* (London: Hogarth Press, 1926). See also note 7.

35. "Books of the Quarter," 751.

36. *Poetry and Criticism*, 23. For Sitwell, Beddoes' "Song" (1851) represents the "nearest approach" to "making abstract poems in words as the modernist poet has."

37. *Poetry and Criticism*, 7–9.

38. Percy Bysshe Shelley, "Peter Bell the Third" (written 1819, published 1839).

39. Samuel Taylor Coleridge, "Youth and Age" (1828).

Chapter 2 T. E. Hulme, the New Barbarism, and Gertrude Stein

1. Riding most likely composed this chapter in response to T. S. Eliot's 1927 review, titled "Charleston, Hey! Hey!," in which he deemed Gertrude Stein's writing an "ominous" harbinger of a "barbarian" future (see n. 8 below). An earlier (and shorter) version of this chapter appeared under the same title in *transition* 3 (June 1927): 153–168. Robert Graves and Riding also reworked some of this material as the "Conclusion" to *A Survey of Modernist Poetry* (London: William Heinemann, 1927).

2. This phrase became widely known after the publication of Ernest Hemingway's *The Sun Also Rises* (1926). In that volume, Hemingway credits Stein with the phrase.

3. After the publication of *The Waste Land* in 1922, Eliot published *The Hollow Men* (1925), "Doris's Dream Songs, I–III" (parts of which were reprinted in *Poems 1909–1935*), and parts of what would later become *Sweeney Agonistes* (1932).

4. "Books of the Quarter," *New Criterion* 4.4 (October 1926), 751.

5. Riding joins Wyndham Lewis in denouncing modernist poetry as Bergsonian. In *Time and Western Man* (1927), Lewis outlines the "psychology of the time-snob" modernist, who glorifies "life-in-the-moment, with no reference . . . to absolute or universal value." Lewis also discusses modernists' desire to "return to the Past," in the form of the child or the primitive. Riding's critical terms are similar to Lewis's, but she reverses his dismissal of Gertrude Stein's *Composition as Explanation*. See Wyndham Lewis, *Time & Western Man* [1927] (Santa Rosa: Black Sparrow Press, 1993), 11, 14, 35, 59–63.

6. Most of T. E. Hulme's essays on poetry, sculpture, painting, philosophy, and politics initially appeared in *The New Age* journal during the years before

and during World War I. After Hulme's death in the war, Herbert Read collected selections from his writings and notebooks and published them as *Speculations: Essays on Humanism and the Philosophy of Art*, ed. Herbert Read (London: Kegan Paul, Trench, Trubner & Co., 1924).

7. Eliot, "Commentary," *Criterion* II (April 1924): 231.

8. "Charleston, Hey! Hey!," *Nation & Athenaeum*, 40:17 (29 January 1927): 595.

9. "Romanticism and Classicism," *Speculations*, 126.

10. *The Profanity of Paint* (London: A. C. Fifield, 1916).

11. *Gaudier-Brzeska: A Memoir* (London: John Lane, 1916), 137–138.

12. *Gaudier-Brzeska*, 138.

13. This quotation represents Riding's translation of two lines from Gaudier-Brzeska's manifesto into William Kiddier's non-objectifying prose. The lines from Gaudier-Brzeska's manifesto—which originally appeared in the first issue of *BLAST* (1914)—read, "Sculptural feeling is the appreciation of masses in relation. Sculptural ability is the defining of these masses by planes." *Gaudier-Brzeska*, 138.

14. "Bergson's Theory of Art," in *Speculations*, 147.

15. *White Buildings* (New York: Boni & Liveright, 1926). In his introduction to *White Buildings*, Allen Tate suggests that the "separation of vision and subject" in modern poetry arises because "the poet no longer apprehends his world as a Whole" (xi).

16. "Bergson's Theory of Art," 163.

17. Eliot's "Fragment of a Prologue"—which later became the first part of *Sweeney Agonistes* (1932)—appeared in the *Criterion* 4.4 (October 1926): 713.

18. See Gertrude Stein's 1926 portrait "Jean Cocteau" in *Portraits and Prayers* (New York: Random House, 1934), 81.

19. See Gertrude Stein, *Composition As Explanation* in *A Stein Reader*, ed. Ulla Dydo (Evanston: Northwestern UP, 1993), 495. In the section that follows, Riding cites repeatedly from Stein's *Composition as Explanation*, which was first published in *Dial* 81, no. 4 (October 1926), then delivered as a lecture at Oxford University in June 1926, and finally published in book form by Leonard and Virginia Woolf's Hogarth Press in November of the same year. Riding relies on Stein's sense of the continuous present throughout Chapter 2 of *Contemporaries*, particularly when describing the "time sense" in contemporary poetry, and as she attempts to explain Stein's "barbarism" in terms of her radical deconstruction of language, best demonstrated in *Composition As Explanation*.

20. *Composition As Explanation*, 497.

21. *Composition As Explanation*, 499–500.

22. *Composition As Explanation*, 497.

23. *Composition As Explanation*, 501.

24. Gertrude Stein, *The Making of Americans* (Dijon: Contact Editions, 1925). Though Stein began writing *The Making of Americans* as early as 1903, and finished the manuscript in 1911, it did not appear in print until 1925 and was reviewed by Edith Sitwell for *The Criterion* in 1926, a review Riding certainly would have read.

25. *Composition As Explanation*, 499.

26. Herbert Read, ed., *Speculations: Essays on Humanism and the Philosophy of Art* (London: Kegan Paul, Trench, Trubner & Co., 1924), 34.

27. Stein, *What Are Masterpieces?* (Los Angeles: Conference Press, 1940), 57.

28. Stein, "Jean Cocteau," 84.

29. *Composition As Explanation*, 500.

30. *Composition As Explanation*, 501.

31. *Composition As Explanation*, 502.

Chapter 3 *The Facts in the Case of Monsieur Poe*

1. "The Facts in the Case of Monsieur Poe" likewise appeared in altered form previous to its inclusion in *Contemporaries*, first as a lecture before the Oxford English Club in March of 1927, then as an essay entitled "Jamais Plus" that appeared in the October 1927 issue of *transition* (139–56). Elizabeth Friedmann indicates that Riding's lecture at Oxford was presented as a preview of a chapter from *Contemporaries*, "in which she explained how the myth of Edgar Allan Poe's genius became so widely held and long maintained. She portrayed the icon of the French *symbolists* not as America's greatest literary genius but as a self-publicizing hack journalist who wrote 'literary rush orders' to produce a predetermined effect." See *A Mannered Grace: The Life of Laura (Riding) Jackson*, 103.

2. Riding draws these unattributed quotations from Yale Professor Carl Schrieber's article "A Close-Up of Poe" that appeared in the *Saturday Review of Literature* 3.11 (October 9, 1926): 165–67.

3. Edgar Allan Poe, "To Helen" (1831).

4. "Edgar Allan Poe," *In the American Grain* (New York: New Directions, 1956 [1925]), 216–34.

5. "Edgar Allan Poe," 216.

6. James Russell Lowell, "Fable for Critics" (1848).

7. *On a Certain Condescension in Foreigners* (1914).

8. Poe, "Eulalie" (1845).

9. Poe, *Bon-Bon* (1850).

10. Poe, "The Rationale of Verse" (1848).

11. "Edgar Allan Poe," 216–34.

12. Poe, "To One in Paradise" (1834).

13. Riding most likely refers to Eliot's "Note sur Mallarmé et Poe," *La Nouvelle Révue Française* 14 (November 1, 1926), 524–26.

14. "Edgar Allan Poe," 222.

15. Riding cites a letter from Poe to T. W. White, April 30, 1835. The full sentence reads: "I noticed the allusion in the Doom. The writer seems to compare my swim with that of Lord Byron, whereas there can be no comparison between them."

16. From the preface to Poe's *Tamerlane and Other Poems* (1827).

17. From the preface to (George Gordon) Lord Byron's *Hours of Idleness* (1807), his first collection of poems.

18. Riding refers to Poe's 1846 essay, "The Philosophy of Composition," which elaborates a strict formula for poetic composition, using "The Raven" as an ideal example.

19. Thomas Moore, "To the Boston Frigate, On Leaving Halifax for England" (1804).

20. *A Defense of Poetry* (1821).

21. *The Poetic Principle* (1850).

22. William Motherwell, "The Cavalier's Song" (1841).

23. "The Philosophy of Composition" (1846).

24. See Malcolm Cowley's preface to his translation of Paul Valéry's *Variété* (New York: Harcourt, Brace & Co., 1927).

25. "Note sur Mallarmé et Poe," 524–26.

26. "The Philosophy of Composition" (1846).

27. A typographical error—Riding refers here to American writer and artist, Christopher Pearse Cranch (1813–1892).

28. "The beautiful cries of real passion, the elegance of love . . ." comes from the preface to Edgar Allan Poe, *Poésies Complètes*, trans. Gabriel Mourey (Paris: Mercure de France, 1910), 1.

29. "Baudelaire, Mallarmé, Hennequin, Rollinat, yourself and others. . . ." *Poésies Complètes*, 5.

30. "We have done so much in France to acclimate Edgar Poe that his compatriots insist that the author of 'The Raven' was French." John H. Ingram, letter to Gabriel Mourey, as quoted in the preface to Mourey's translation of Poe. *Poésies Complètes*, 5.

31. "Poe loved France and its admirable literature and only spoke with respect of the masterpieces that it produced; his caustic pen would never try to diminish its glory." *Poésies Complètes*, 6.

32. From Mourey's 1910 French translation of Edgar Allan Poe's "The Raven" (1845). *Poésies Complètes*, 21. The stanza in English reads:

"Prophet!" said I, "thing of evil!—prophet still, if bird or devil!
Whether Tempter sent, or whether tempest tossed thee here ashore,
Desolate, yet all undaunted, on this desert land enchanted—
On this home by Horror haunted,—tell me truly, I implore—
Is there—is there balm in Giliad?—tell me—tell me, I implore!"
Quoth the Raven, "Nevermore."

Chronological Bibliography

As Laura Riding

The Close Chaplet. London: Hogarth Press, 1926.

[with Robert Graves]. *A Survery of Modernist Poetry*. London: Heinemann, 1927. Reprint, New York: Haskell House, 1969. Reprint, Manchester: Carcanet, 2002.

Voltaire: A Biographical Fantasy. London: Hogarth Press, 1927.

Anarchism Is Not Enough. London: Jonathan Cape, 1928. Reprint, Berkeley: University of California Press, 2001.

Contemporaries and Snobs. New York: Doubleday, Duran, & Co., 1928. Reprint, St. Clair Shore: Scholarly Press, 1971.

A Pamphlet Against Anthologies. New York: Doubleday, Duran, & Co., 1928. Reprint, New York: AMS, 1970. Reprint, Manchester: Carcanet, 2002.

Experts Are Puzzled. London: Jonathan Cape, 1930.

Four Unposted Letters to Catherine. Paris: Hours, 1930. Reprint, New York: Persea, 1993.

Poems: A Joking Word. London: Jonathan Cape, 1930.

Though Gently. Deya: Seizin Press, 1930.

Twenty Poems Less. Paris: Hours, 1930.

Laura and Francisca. Deya: Seizin Press, 1931.

Everybody's Letters. London: Barker, 1933.

The Life of the Dead. London: Barker, 1933.

Poet: A Lying Word. London: Barker, 1933.

Americans. Los Angeles: Primavera, 1934.

[with George Ellidge]. *14A*. London: Barker, 1934.

Progress of Stories. London: Constable, 1935. Reprint, New York: Dial, 1982. Reprint, New York: Persea, 1994.

The Second Leaf (broadside). Deya: Seizin Press, 1935.

[Madeleine Vara, pseud.] *Convalescent Conversations*. Deya: Seizen Press, 1936.
[Edited with Robert Graves.] *Epilogue* I. London: Constable, 1936.
———. *Epilogue* II. London: Constable, 1936.
———. *Epilogue* III. London: Constable, 1937.
A Trojan Ending. London: Constable, 1937. Reprint, Manchester: Carcanet, 1984.
Collected Poems. London: Cassell; New York: Random House, 1938.
The Covenant of Literal Morality. London: Seizin Press, 1938.
The World and Ourselves. London: Chatto & Windus, 1938.
Lives of Wives. New York: Random House, 1939. Reprint, Los Angeles: Sun and Moon, 1995. Reprint, Los Angeles: Sun and Moon, 2000.
Selected Poems in Five Sets. New York: Persea, 1993.

As Laura (Riding) Jackson

The Telling. London: Athlowe, 1972; New York: Harper & Row, 1973. Reprint, Manchester: Fyfield Books, 2005.
"What, If Not a Poem, Poems?" *Denver Quarterly* 9.2 (1974): 1–13.
"Dr. Grove and the Future of the English Dictionaries." *Denver Quarterly* 10.1 (spring 1975). Reprinted in *Rational Meaning*.
"On Ambiguity." *Modern Language Quarterly* 36.1 (March 1975): 102–106. Reprinted in *Rational Meaning*.
"Bertrand Russell, and Others: The Idea of the Master-Mind." *Antaeus* 21/22 (spring–summer 1976): 125–35.
"It Has Taken Too Long: From the Writings of Laura (Riding) Jackson." *Chelsea* 35 (1976): entire issue.
Description of Life. New York: Oliphant, 1980.
The Poems of Laura Riding: A New Edition of the 1938 Collection. New York: Persea, 1980.
Some Communications of Broad Reference. Northridge: Lord John, 1983.
"Engaging the Impossible." *Sulfur* 10 (1984): 4–35.
"As to a Certain Poem & Poetry" ("Lamenting the Terms of Modern Praise"). *Chelsea* 47 (1988): 3–5.
First Awakenings: The Early Poems of Laura Riding. New York: Persea, 1992.
The Word "Woman" and Other Related Writings. Edited by Elizabeth Friedmann and Alan J. Clark. New York: Persea, 1993.
"About the Fugitives and Myself." *The Carolina Quarterly* 47.3 (summer 1995): 73–87.
"The Promise of Words." *London Review of Books* 7 (September 1995): 23–24.
[with Schuyler B. Jackson]. *Rational Meaning: A New Foundation for the Defi-*

nition of Words. Edited by William Harmon. Introduction by Charles Bernstein. Charlottesville: University Press of Virginia, 1997.

The Sufficient Difference: A Centenary Celebration of Laura (Riding) Jackson. Edited by Elizabeth Friedmann. New York: Chelsea Associates, 2000.

[with Robert Graves]. *Essays from* Epilogue *1935–1937*. Manchester: Carcanet, 2001.

The Poems of Laura Riding: A Newly Revised Edition of the 1938/1980 Collection. New York: Persea, 2001.

Laura Riding, Gertrude Stein, Jane Bowles. Warsaw: Wydaje Biblioteka Narodowa, 2003.

"Literature and the Right." *Delmar* 10 (2004): 69-81.

Under the Mind's Watch: Concerning Issues of Language, Literature, Life of Contemporary Bearing. Edited by John Nolan and Alan J. Clark. Bern: Peter Lang, 2004.

The Laura (Riding) Jackson Reader. Edited by Elizabeth Freidmann. New York: Persea, 2005.

The Failure of Poetry, the Promise of Language (Poets on Poetry). Ann Arbor: University of Michigan Press, 2007.

On the Continuing of the Continuing. London: Wyeswood Press, 2008.

[with Jan Erik Bouman]. *As Many Questions As Answers*. Den Haag: Bureau Claxon, 2010.

The Person I Am: The Literary Memoirs of Laura (Riding) Jackson, Volume One. Edited by John Nolan and Carol Ann Friedmann. Nottingham: Trent Editions, 2011.

The Person I Am: The Literary Memoirs of Laura (Riding) Jackson, Volume Two. Edited by John Nolan and Carol Ann Friedmann. Nottingham: Trent Editions, 2011.

Index of Names

Aiken, Conrad, 18
Aldrich, Mary A. S., 109
Allan, John, 98
Anderson, Sherwood, 27
Archimedes, 58
Aristotle, 44, 49, 62, 66

Barrett, Elizabeth Barrett (Elizabeth Barrett Browning), 103
Barrie, J. M., 38
Baudelaire, 9 (cited in Waste Land) 37, 77, 111, 114n6, 120n29
Beddoes, Thomas Lovell, 42, 117n36
Beerbohm, Max, 38
Beowulf, 52
Bergson, Henri, 78, 118
Blake, William, 19
Bonaparte, Napoleon, 69
Boone, Daniel, 92
Borrow, George, 21, 27
Bradley, F. H., 49
Branch, Christopher Pease, 89, 109, 120n27
Bridges, Robert, 43
Brontë, Charlotte, 20
Browne, Thomas, 19
Bryant, William Cullen, 88, 89, 90, 104
Butler, Samuel, 37
Byron, George Gordon Lord, 10, 89, 97, 99, 120n17

Campbell, Roy, 18
Carpenter, Edward, 37
Chapman, George, 111
Chaucer, Geoffrey, 2
Clemm, Virginia, 98
Cocteau, Jean, 15–16, 27, 115nn18–19, 118n18, 119n28
Coleridge, Samuel Taylor, 20, 44, 101, 117n39
Collins, William, 19
Cowley, Abraham, 11, 114nn10–11
Cowley, Malcolm, 108, 120n24
Cowper, William, xxiii, 19
Craik, Dinah, 20
Cranch, Christopher Pearse, 89. *See* Branch, Christoper Pease
Crane, Hart, x, xi, xvi, 14, 77, 115n15
Cummings, E. E., xi, 14, 32, 48
Cunard, Nancy, 13

Dana, Charles A., 88
Darwin, Erasmus, 12, 114n13
Darwin, Charles, 69
Davidson, John, 38
Denham, Sir John, 19
DeQuincey, Thomas, 43, 96–97
Dickens, Charles, 102, 110
Diodorus Siculus, 40
Disraeli, Benjamin, 20
Donne, John, 3, 11, 16, 108
Doughty, Charles Montagu, 37
Dowson, Ernest, 38
Dryden, John, 3, 11, 99, 114n8

Einstein, Albert, 48–49, 58, 114n4
Eliot, T. S., x–xiii, xv–xvii, xix, xxi, xxiii, 8–10, 24–28, 31, 41, 44–45, 48, 55–

56, 58–59, 66, 77–80, 93, 108, 110–112, 113n1, 114nn5–6, 116n26, 117n1, 117n3, 118n7, 118n17, 120n130
Emerson, Ralph Waldo, 90
Euripides, 58

Fernandez, M. Ramon, 25–27, 116n22, 116nn25–26
Fielding, Henry, 12
Fletcher, John, 19
Frank, Waldo, 27
Freud, Sigmund, 49

Galsworthy, John, 37
Gaudier-Brzeska, Henri, xv, 72–74, 118nn11–13
Goethe, Johann Wolfgang von, 10, 97
Goldsmith, Oliver, 19
Goodwin, Leslie, xii, 29
Graves, Robert, xii–xiii, xv, xviii, xxi, xxiii, 9, 114n7, 116n29, 117n1
Gray, Thomas, 19
Greene, Robert, 2
Griswold, Rufus Wilmot (Reverend), 88–89

Hardy, Thomas, 37
Hawthorne, Nathaniel, 110
Hennequin, Émile, 111, 120n29
Homer, 99
Hood, Thomas, 89, 105
Horace, 99
Horne, Richard Henry, 109
Howard, Frederick, 100
Hulme, T. E., x, xi, xiii, xv, 35, 51, 63–71, 75–76, 78–79, 83, 117n33, 117–18n6
Huxley, Aldous, 18, 31

Ingram, John H., 111, 120n30

Johnson, Samuel 2, 11, 19, 100–101, 114n10
Joyce, James xi, xv, xvii, 12, 27, 48, 78–79

Keats, John, 19–20, 29–30, 39, 43–44, 71, 97, 106
Kiddier, William, 71–74, 118n13
King, Henry, 111
Kipling, Rudyard, 43

Laforgue, Jules, 31, 37
Lamartine, Alfonse de, 10
Lawrence, D. H., 37
Leonard, William Ellery, 18
Lodge, Thomas, 2
Longfellow, Henry Wadsworth, 88–90, 102–103
Lowell, James Russell, 89–90, 119n6

Mallarmé, Stéphane, 108, 111, 120n13, 120n25, 120n29
Maritain, Jacques, 16, 28, 115nn18–19
Masefield, John, 18
Melville, Herman, 21, 27
Mencken, H. L., 89
Michelangelo, 111
Middleton, Richard, 38
Milton, John, 19, 29
Moore, George, 27
Moore, Marianne, xi, 14, 48
Moore, Thomas, 89, 102, 104, 120n19
Morris, William, 37
Motherwell, William 106, 120n22
Mourey, Gabriel, 111, 120n28, 120n30, 120n32
Muir, Edwin, xv, 9, 26, 113n1, 114n7

Neal, John, 88, 100
Nightingale, Florence, 34
Noyes, Alfred, 18, 43

O'Shaughnessy, Arthur, 38
Ossian, 102
Ovid, 40

Pater, Walter, 40
Peele, George, 2
Philips, Ambrose, 19
Pinkney, Edward C., 88–89, 104
Plato, 48–49
Poe, Edgar Allan, v, xi, 16, 22, 86–112, 119nn1–5, 119nn8–11, 120nn12–16, 120n25, 120n28, 120nn30–32
Pope, Alexander, 3, 4, 11, 19, 29, 114n11, 116n29
Pound, Ezra, xi, xv, xvi, 27, 72–74, 78
Proust, Marcel, 27, 116n29

Ransom, John Crowe, x, xi, 12, 114n12
Read, Herbert, x, 25–27, 116n22, 116nn25–26, 117–18n6, 119n26
Rickword, Edgell, x, 27, 116n27
Rimbaud, Arthur, xv, 4, 14, 16, 86, 97, 111, 113n2, 115n16, 115n19
Robinson, Edwin Arlington, 18
Rochefoucault, François de la, 100
Rollinat, Maurice, 111, 120n29
Rousseau, Jean Jacques, 37, 97
Ruskin, John, 40, 71

Sackville-West, Vita, 18
Sassoon, Siegfried, 12
Scott-Moncrieff, Charles, 27
Shakespeare, William, xi, 2–3, 42
Shanks, Edward, 43
Shelley, Percy Bysshe, 5–6, 20, 43–44, 98, 105–7, 114n3, 116n32, 117n38
Sidney, Sir Philip, 2
Sitwell, Edith, xi, xv, 9, 15, 18, 29–32, 41–44, 48, 80, 113n1, 114n7, 116n29, 117n36, 119n24
Soames, Enoch, 38
Socrates, 111
Spenser, Edmund, 2, 19
Squire, J. C., 43
Stedman, Edmund Clarence, 88
Stein, Gertrude, ix–xi, xiii, xviii–xxii, 32, 51, 55, 66, 78, 80–85, 91, 117nn1–2, 117n5 118nn18–22, 119nn23–25, 119nn27–31
Symons, Arthur, 37

Tate, Allen, x, xi, xv, 77–78, 113n1, 114–15n14, 118n15
Tennyson, Alfred Lord, 7, 10, 29, 43, 89, 102, 105
Thompson, Francis, 35, 116n32
Thomson, James [*Bysshe Vanolis*], 38
Turner, W. J., 18

Valéry, Paul, 6, 15, 22, 32, 108, 115n17, 120n24
Verlaine, Paul, 97, 111
Virgil, 19

Warens, Françoise-Louise de, 96
Welby, Amelia, 89, 109
Wells, H. G., 37
Whitman, Walt, 29
Williams, William Carlos, 89–93
Willis, Nathaniel Parker, 88, 10, 109
Woolf, Virginia, xi, 27, 113n1, 118n19
Wordsworth, William, xi, 20, 29–31, 43–44, 101–2